Access to A-Level History

General Editor: Keith Randell

alin an Khrushchev: he USSR, 1924–64

:hael Lynch

lodder & Stoughton

LONDON SYDNEY AUCKLAND TORONTO

The cover illustration shows Stalin and Khrushchev together. (Courtesey Popperfoto)

British Library Cataloguing in Publication Data
Lynch, Michael, *1946– Aug 22–*
  Stalin to Krushchev: USSR 1924–1964.—(Access to A-
level history
  1. Soviet Union, 1917
  I. Title   II. Series
  947.084

ISBN 0 340 525592

First published 1990

Typeset by Wearside Tradespools, Fulwell, Sunderland
Printed in Great Britain for the educational publishing division of Hodder and Stoughton
Ltd, Mill Road, Dunton Green, Sevenoaks, Kent by Page Bros (Norwich) Ltd.

Contents

CHAPTER 1   Introduction: The USSR, 1924–64   1
1 Background   1
2 Stalin and Khrushchev   2
3 The Basic Problems for the USSR, 1924–64   3
Study Guides   4

CHAPTER 2   Stalin: The Rise to Power   8
1 Background   8
2 The Roots of Stalin's Power   10
3 Stalin versus Trotsky   14
a) The NEP   18
b) Socialism in One Country   19
4 The Defeat of Trotsky and the Left   20
5 The Defeat of the Right   22
Study Guides   24

CHAPTER 3   Stalin and the Soviet Economy   28
1 Background   28
2 Collectivisation   30
3 Industrialisation   35
a) The First Five-Year Plan   36
b) The Second and Third Five-Year Plans   41
4 The Economy During Wartime, 1941–45   43
5 Postwar Reconstruction   46
Study Guides   47

CHAPTER 4   Stalin and Political Power   52
1 The Earlier Purges   52
2 The Post-Kirov Purges, 1934–36   53
3 The Great Purge, 1936–39   56
a) The Purge of the Party   56
b) The Purge of the Army   59
c) The Purge of the People   60
4 The Later Purges, 1941–53   61
5 The Dimensions of the Purges   63
6 The Purges in Perspective   64
Study Guides   66

CHAPTER 5   Stalin and International Relations   70
1 Introduction   70
2 Soviet Foreign Policy, 1924–29   72
a) Anglo-Soviet Relations   72

b) Stalin and International Communism   74
3 Soviet Foreign Policy, 1929–33   76
4 Soviet Foreign Policy, 1933–39   77
5 The Nazi–Soviet Pact, 1939–41   80
6 The Grand Alliance, 1941–45   84
7 The Cold War   87
Study Guides   91

CHAPTER 6   Khrushchev   95
1 Early Career   95
2 Rise to Power   96
3 De-Stalinisation   98
4 De-Stalinisation and the Soviet Satellites   102
5 Khrushchev and the Soviet Economy   103
a) Agriculture   103
b) Industry   105
6 Co-existence   106
7 Khrushchev and Germany   108
8 The Cuban Missile Crisis   112
9 Khrushchev and China   113
10 The Fall of Khrushchev   115
Study Guides   118

CHAPTER 7   The Soviet Record, 1924–64   122
1 The Exercise of Power   122
2 The Economy   125
3 Foreign Relations   127
Study Guides   130

Further Reading   134

Glossary   136

Sources on Stalin and Khrushchev   137

Index   138

Preface

To the teacher

The *Access to A-Level History* series has been planned with the A-level student specifically in mind. The text of each volume has been made sufficiently expansive to allow the reader to complete a section without needing to re-read paragraphs in order to 'unpack' condensed narrative or to 'tease out' obscure meanings. The amount of factual detail is suitable for the requirements of A-level, and care has been taken to ensure that all the 'facts' included have been explained or placed in context so as to allow proper understanding. Differing interpretations of events are discussed as appropriate and extracts from sources are woven into the main text. This is essential if A-level students are to be encouraged to argue a case, bringing in suitable evidence to substantiate their points. The hope is that the text will be sufficiently interesting to increase student motivation towards reading history books, and sufficiently stimulating to encourage students to think analytically about what they have learnt.

It is also intended that the series will offer direct assistance to students in preparing to answer both essay and source-based questions. It is expected that the help with source-based questions will be particularly welcomed. The sections providing guidance to the student which appear at the end of each chapter could be used either as a basis for class discussion or by students when working on their own. Direct help is also given with note making and realistic suggestions are made for further reading.

To the student

Many of you will find that this suggested procedure will enable you to derive the most benefit from each book:

1. Read a whole chapter as fast as you can, and preferably in one sitting.
2. Study the flow diagram at the end of the chapter, ensuring that you understand the general pattern of events covered.
3. Study the 'Answering essay questions on . . .' section at the end of the chapter, consciously identifying the major issues involved.
4. Read the 'Making notes on . . .' section at the end of the chapter, and decide on the pattern of notes you will make.
5. Read the chapter a second time, stopping at each * or chapter sub-heading to make notes on what you have just read.
6. Attempt the 'Source-based questions on . . .' section at the end of the chapter.

When you have finished the book decide whether you need to do further reading on the topic. This will be important if you are seriously aspiring to a high grade at A-level. The 'Further Reading' section at the end of the book will help you decide what to choose.

I wish you well with your A-level studies. I hope they are both enjoyable and successful. If you can think of any ways in which this book could be more useful to students please write to me with your suggestions.

Keith Randell

Acknowledgements

The publishers would like to thank the following for permission to reproduce material in this volume:

Svetlana Alliluyeva for the extract from her book *Twenty Letters to a Friend*, Century Hutchinson (1986); The Bodley Head for the extract from *Stalin* by Leon Trotsky, published by Hollis and Carter (1947); Jonathan Cape Ltd for the extract from *Eastern Approaches* by Fitzroy MacLean (1951); The Daily Telegraph for the extract from *The Daily Telegraph*, 24 November, 1988; Lawrence & Wishart Ltd for the extracts from J V Stalin 'Works' Volumes 6 and 13 (1953); MacDonald and Co (Publishers) Ltd for the extracts from *Purnell's History of the Twentieth Century* (1968); MacMillan Ltd and The University of North Carolina Press for the extract from *Stalinist Planning for Economic Growth 1933–52* by E Zaleski (1980); Roger Morgan for the extracts from his book *The Unsettled Peace*, BBC Books (1979); The Observer for the extract from 'Stalin' by E Crankshaw, *The Observer Magazine*, 27 May, 1979; Oxford University Press for the extracts from *Memoirs of a Revolutionary 1901–41* by V Serge, translated by Peter Sedgwick (1963), *The Prophet Armed: Trotsky 1921–9* by I Deutscher (1970) and *Endurance and Endeavour* by J N Westwood (1985); Penguin Books Ltd for the extracts from *Lenin* by D Shub (1966) and *An Economic History of the USSR* by A Nove (1976); John Scott for the extract from his book *Behind the Urals*, Secker and Warburg (1942); Unwin Hyman Ltd for the extracts from *Stalinism and After* by Alec Nove (1975).

Every effort has been made to trace and acknowledge ownership of copyright. The publishers will be glad to make suitable arrangements with any copyright holders whom it has not been possible to contact.

The publishers would like to thank the following for permission to reproduce copyright illustrations:

The Trustees of the British Museum, 39; Daily Express/Solo Syndication, 82; London University (School of Slavonic and East European Studies), 99.

CHAPTER 1

Introduction: The USSR, 1924–64

1 Background

The Russian Revolution of 1917 is arguably the most significant, and certainly the most controversial, happening of the twentieth century. According to the revolutionaries then, and supporters of the Revolution since, what took place in Russia in 1917 was nothing less than the taking of power by the people and the creation of a new state and society in which the workers ruled. This interpretation asserts that Lenin, applying the revolutionary theories of Karl Marx, led the Bolshevik (Communist) Party to victory on behalf of the masses. During the next three years the Bolsheviks had to defend their revolution against the forces of reaction (generally referred to as the Whites) and to fight off attempted invasions of Soviet Russia by the Western capitalist powers. They were successful in this; by the time of Lenin's death in 1924, his Bolshevik Party had laid the basis for the development of the USSR as the world's first truly socialist state. Soviet Russia thus became the leader of – and the model for – all other nations and peoples who aspired to revolutionary change.

Essential to this Marxist analysis of what happened between 1917 and 1924 is the view that the Russian Revolution was a unique event in history. Marxists, who believe that human history is explained by the class war, contend that 1917 marked the beginning of the world-wide rising of the proletariat (the exploited working class) against the bourgeoisie (the exploiting capitalist class). The inevitable triumph of the workers of the world had begun.

*Non-Marxist observers reject the idea of inevitability in history. They see the Russian Revolution in a different light. Critics of Bolshevism stress how small-scale the October rising had been. They accept that its consequences were of great significance but they dismiss the interpretation of it as a mass movement. They describe it, instead, as an opportunist Bolshevik coup, which succeeded not because of the masses who supported it, but because of the weakness of the Provisional Government against which it was directed. Far from being a seizure of power *by* the masses, the October Revolution was a seizure of power *from* the masses. This was proved by the violent dispersal in January 1918 of the Constituent Assembly, the only democratically elected national body in Russian history. The repression, which characterised the Bolsheviks' consolidation of their power, was to remain the outstanding feature of subsequent Soviet rule.

Those who hold this view find support for it in the failure of

See Preface for explanation of * symbol.

revolution to spread elsewhere in Europe. It had been Lenin's belief that once the spark of revolution ignited in Russia the flame would spread across the neighbouring states. This did not happen. Brief glimmerings of revolution in Germany and Hungary were soon extinguished. When Bolshevik forces entered Poland in 1920, the Poles reacted as nationalists, not as revolutionary class brothers, and drove out the Red Army which had come to 'liberate' them. Soviet Russia found itself the only revolutionary state in a hostile, capitalist, world.

*Between these two schools of thought – the one extolling the virtues of the Revolution as a great liberating force, the other condemning it as an intrinsically oppressive movement – there is a variety of interpretations, supportive, critical and neutral. That the Russian Revolution should continue to excite such interest among historians and political commentators shows how important the subject is held to be. The closing words of the Communist Manifesto, the equivalent of a Marxist bible, called on proletarian revolutionaries to fight for 'the forcible overthrow of all existing social conditions'. The Russian Bolsheviks took up this cry and appealed to the workers in all countries to rise against their governments. In 1919 the Bolsheviks created the Comintern (Communist International) for the specific purpose of organising revolution worldwide. The threat to the established order in Europe and elsewhere was very clear. No country could look upon Soviet Russia as other than a potential enemy. The mutual hostility that this engendered continued for the whole of the period 1924–64. A further factor explaining the fierceness of the debate about modern Russian history is that since the 1920s there has been a deep division among Communists themselves over the true nature of the Revolution after Lenin. All Communists accept Lenin as the infallible interpreter of Marxist theory and as the father of the Russian Revolution.

2 Stalin and Khrushchev

There is no such unanimity of opinion about the role of Lenin's successors. The period 1924–64 was dominated by Stalin while he lived, and by the shadow he cast after his death in 1953. During the last thirty years of his life, 1924–53, Stalin took on heroic proportions in the eyes of the Soviet people. He presented himself to them as the heir of the great Lenin, the creator of a modern economy, the destroyer of the country's internal enemies, the warrior who led the nation to victory over fascism, and the leader who successfully guided his country into the nuclear age. Yet, only three years after his death, Stalin's god-like reputation began to be destroyed. His successor, Khrushchev (Soviet leader 1956–64), initiated a programme of 'de-Stalinisation', during which a whole list of crimes against the Communist Party were levelled at him. Khrushchev's main charge was that Stalin had strayed from the path of true Marxism–Leninism by creating his own 'cult of personality'. Khrushchev's attack on Stalin for his gross misuse of personal power did more than simply challenge the reputation of a past leader; it had the effect of raising doubts about the record of the Soviet Union as a revolutionary state. How could a truly Marxist system have allowed itself to be abused in this way? From that basic question arose a number of queries about the development of Soviet Communism after Lenin. The most insistent of these was whether Stalin had fulfilled or betrayed the Revolution begun by Lenin in 1917. The issue was of major importance. If the Bolshevik rising of 1917 was, indeed, the first truly proletarian revolution, and if Lenin was the founder of the first Marxist state, how was Stalin to be judged? Did he fulfil Lenin's work or did he destroy it? Was Stalinism a logical extension of the system Lenin had established or a perversion of it? Did the policy of de-Stalinisation that Khrushchev introduced in the 1950s, merely blacken Stalin's reputation or did it introduce real changes into the Soviet system? Such questions indicate some of the major issues with which historians concern themselves when they analyse Soviet history.

3 The Basic Problems for the USSR, 1924–64

It is by a questioning approach that one may begin to develop an understanding of the period covered by this book. There are three basic questions that together indicate the main determinants of the USSR's development in the years 1924–64 and which suggest the areas of historical debate.

a) How would power be exercised in the Soviet state, and by whom?

In 1924 this was still undecided. Before they came to power in 1917, Lenin and the Bolsheviks had simply assumed that a successful proletarian revolution would lead to a withering away of the State. However, for most of the period 1917–24 they found themselves fighting for sheer survival. As a consequence, the Bolsheviks became increasingly authoritarian. They outlawed their political rivals and greatly increased the size and scope of government. Would this go on? Would the Soviet Union return to establishing the freedoms that had inspired many of the revolutionaries of 1917 or would it continue its drift towards totalitarianism? Who would actually hold power?

b) How would the economy develop under Soviet Communism?

The Russian economy was taken over by the Bolsheviks in 1917 with the idea of transforming it from a capitalist to a socialist system. Lenin directed that a start be made towards bringing industry under direct Bolshevik control as a first stage in the centralisation of the economy.

This was possible with industry, but agriculture proved a different matter. The Great War, the Revolution in 1917, and the Civil War that followed, had disrupted food production and distribution to the point where Russia was starving. In 1921, in an effort to prevent famine, Lenin introduced the New Economic Policy (NEP). This was a concession to the peasants. It allowed them to keep their surplus produce and sell it at a profit. Lenin readily admitted that this was a return to capitalist methods, but he argued that the move was justified by the desperate circumstances. The NEP worked in the short term; the peasants responded by producing more food for the nation. The question that Lenin left to his successors was how long should the NEP be continued. A serious division in Party thinking occurred over this. There were those, who became known as the Left Bolsheviks, who regarded the NEP as being contrary to true socialism and wanted it abandoned. They were opposed by the Right Bolsheviks, who considered that the Policy should be maintained for as long as it continued to provide food. How would Stalin respond to this issue? How would he interpret the Soviet Union's agricultural and industrial needs, and by what methods would he attempt to satisfy them?

c) What were to be the relations of the Soviet Union with the outside world?

For the Bolsheviks, this had been more than simply a question of foreign policy. In accordance with their Marxist beliefs, they had expected their seizure of power in Russia to be quickly followed by world revolution. But this did not happen; revolution did not spread. What, then, should Soviet Russia's policy be in a world that resolutely refused to copy the Bolshevik model? Should the Soviet Union still commit itself to the cause of international revolution or should it settle for its own internal consolidation and national development? That was the problem to which Lenin's successors had to address themselves in their conduct of Soviet foreign policy.

It was these three fundamental questions and the response of Stalin and Khrushchev to them that gave shape to the period 1924–64.

Making notes on 'The USSR, 1924–64'

The following chronology will help to give you an idea of the shape of developments in the period. You will not, of course, recognise all the events listed, but if you keep it as a frame of reference you will find it useful as you work through the chapters in the book. You may care to construct a similar time-scale of your own, which you can expand and modify as you go along. It is important not to become lost in detail. Reference to a structured outline helps to prevent this.

1924	**THE USSR**	1964
	Domestic Politics	**Foreign Politics**
1924	Death of Lenin	USSR recognised as sovereign state
1924–29	Power Struggle, Left v Right	Comintern active
	Stalin defeats both	Strained relations with UK, Poland and China

Stalin opts for 'Socialism in One Country'

1928	First Five Year Plan	
1929	Collectivisation begins	'Left turn' – Comintern attacks 'social fascism'
1932–33	Famine	
1933	Second FYP	Hitler in power
1934	Purges begin	USSR joins League of Nations
1936–39	The Great Purges	USSR seeks alliances
1938	Third FYP	Munich Agreement
1939		The Nazi–Soviet Pact

1941–45 The Great Patriotic War

		Yalta and Potsdam Conferences
		USSR a world power, acquires East European satellites
1945		Cold War begins
1946	Fourth FYP	
1947	Leningrad Purge	Truman Doctrine and Marshall Plan
1948		Berlin Blockade,
1949	Soviet A-bomb	NATO, Mao's victory in China
1950		Korean War begins
1951	Fifth FYP	

1953 Death of Stalin

1953–56	Collective Leadership The 'Thaw'	Anti-Soviet demonstrations in E. Germany and Poland
1954	Khrushchev's Virgin Lands Policy	
1955	Sixth FYP	Austrian Peace Treaty

1956	Khrushchev delivers 'Secret Speech' De-Stalinisation begins	Hungarian Rising 'Co-existence'
1957	Khrushchev defeats 'anti-Party Group'	
1958	Khrushchev Premier	Soviet ultimatum on Berlin
1959	Seven-Year Plan	Running dispute with China
1961		Berlin Wall
1962	Disastrous harvest	Cuban Missile Crisis

1964 Khrushchev dismissed

Summary – the period 1924–64

Obviously, at this stage, there will be many terms and ideas that are new to you. Try not to let this worry or confuse you. You will find that as you go about your work systematically, building up your notes section by section and chapter by chapter, your knowledge will keep pace with the demands placed upon it.

In making your own notes on this introductory chapter, the following headings, sub-headings and questions should assist in understanding the issues.

1   Background
1.1 The continuing importance of the Russian Revolution of 1917
1.2 Explain the Marxist interpretation of the 1917 Revolution. How does this affect attitudes towards the period 1924–64?

2   Stalin and Khrushchev
2.1 What image of himself did Stalin present to the Soviet people in this period?
2.2 How did 'de-Stalinisation' subsequently challenge this image?

3   The Basic Problems
3.1 The three key issues shaping the period 1924–64:
   a) The structure and use of state power
   b) The development of the Soviet economy
   c) The Soviet Union's foreign relations

Answering essay questions on 'The USSR, 1924–64'

Questions covering all forty years are less frequent than ones concentrating on particular aspects; however, they do occur, so you are advised to prepare for them. It is also a very useful exercise at this stage to test your understanding of the shape of the period by posing yourself the following type of outline question:

'Examine the main problems facing the Soviet Union and its leaders in the period 1924 to 1964.'

The important word in the question is 'Examine'. It needs to be stressed very strongly that, at A-level, you will hardly ever be asked simply to describe *what* happened; invariably, the questions will be about *why* things happened. In nearly all questions there are key words such as 'analyse', 'explain' or, as here, 'examine'. In responding to these directions, it is never enough for you merely to write down information. A-level requires that you structure and shape your information to meet the terms of the particular question with which you are dealing. The following approach suggests a way of doing this:

1 Begin with a short introductory paragraph describing the approach you are intending to follow. Questions asking for analysis or examination of a whole period are best dealt with by indicating what the basic problems were. This can be done by a straightforward reference to the political, economic and foreign policy issues. It is safe to say that these three categories embrace all the vital factors.

2 A paragraph on the political problems should refer to the situation in revolutionary Russia in 1924 and how it developed during the next forty years. The limits of space and time clearly require that this be done as a set of broad points. Too much detail will bog you down.

3 A similar style paragraph on the economy is called for, suggesting the character of the economic issues in the Soviet Union (1924–64) and the policies adopted in regard to them.

4 A further main paragraph on foreign affairs should follow the same pattern. As you could not hope to cover such a wide-ranging theme in detail, it is even more important here that you restrict yourself to essentials. An effective method of doing this is to define basic foreign-policy objectives, and then to suggest how far you think these were achieved.

5 Always aim to leave yourself enough time for a concluding paragraph. You can use this to emphasise the major points you have tried to make, thus showing your awareness of what 'examine' or 'analyse' demanded of you. A recommended way of rounding off your essay, leaving the examiner with a good impression of you, is to include a brief but apt quotation.

CHAPTER 2

Stalin: The Rise to Power

1 Background

Stalin was not his real name. It was simply the last in a series of aliases that Joseph Vissarionovich Djugashvili adopted in order to avoid detection as a revolutionary in pre-1917 Imperial Russia. Stalin means 'man of steel'. There is much that is obscure about Stalin's early life. As a revolutionary in Tsarist Russia he spent a large part of his time in hiding and in exile. This means that there are many gaps in the story of his younger days. Nevertheless, the main features can be identified. He was born in 1879 in Georgia, a wild and rugged province in the south of the Russian Empire, renowned for the fierceness of its people. Blood feuds and family vendettas were common. Georgia had only recently been incorporated into the Russian Empire. Tsarist government officials often wrote in exasperation of the difficulties of trying to control a savage people who refused to accept their subordination to Russia.

Stalin came from such stock. His father eked out a miserable existence as a shoe-maker and the family appears to have lived in constant poverty. It has been suggested that both Stalin's admiration of things Russian and his contempt for middle-class intellectuals derived from his consciousness of his humble origins. As is common in unsophisticated societies, the Georgians were markedly religious. Stalin's mother was a particularly devout woman and it was largely through her influence that her son was enrolled as a student, training for the priesthood in a Georgian–Orthodox seminary in Tbilisi (Tiflis). It should not be assumed that this denoted any great religious fervour on Stalin's part. At this time in Imperial Russia, attendance at a church establishment was the only way to obtain a Russian-style education, an essential requirement for anyone from the provinces who had ambition. Stalin seems to have been a competent but by no means brilliant student, who was attracted less by theology than by the political ideas with which he came into contact.

*In the seminary records for 1899 there is an entry beside Stalin's name that reads 'expelled for not attending lessons – reasons unknown'. The reasons were in fact that he had become involved in the Georgian resistance movement which was agitating against Tsarist control. His anti-government activities drew him into the Social Democratic Workers Party. This was the Marxist party that in 1903 split into two opposed groups: the Mensheviks, led by Plekhanov, and the Bolsheviks, led by Lenin. From the time of his expulsion from the seminary to the Revolution of 1917 Stalin was a committed follower of Lenin. He threw himself into the task of raising funds for the Bolsheviks; this involved a series of bank and train robberies. To the authorities he was just another Georgian bandit. By 1917 he had been arrested eight times and had been sentenced to periods of imprisonment and exile. These privations further toughened his already hardened character. Afterwards he tended to despise those revolutionaries who had escaped such experiences by fleeing to the relative comfort of self-imposed exile abroad.

Stalin spent the war years, 1914–17, in exile in Siberia. He returned to Petrograd in March 1917, under the amnesty for political prisoners that followed the February Revolution. He had played no part in either the war or the February Revolution, but his efforts in the Bolshevik cause had already brought him to Lenin's notice. Before 1917 the Bolshevik Party was only a few thousand strong and Lenin knew the great majority of members personally. He had been impressed by Stalin's organising ability and willingness to obey orders. He described Stalin as 'that wonderful Georgian', a reference to his revolutionary work among the non-Russian peoples. Lenin showed his favour by having Stalin promoted. By 1912 Stalin had risen to become one of the six members of the Central Committee, the policy making body of the Bolshevik Party. He had also helped to found the Party's newspaper, *Pravda* (Russian for 'Truth').

*Stalin's role in the October Revolution is difficult to disentangle. Official accounts, written after he had taken power, were a mixture of distortion and invention, with any unflattering episodes totally omitted. What is reasonably certain is that Stalin was basically loyal to Lenin after the latter's return to Petrograd in April, 1917. Lenin instructed the Bolsheviks to abandon all co-operation with other parties and to devote themselves to preparing for a take-over of power. As one of Lenin's loyal followers, Stalin was opposed to the 'October Deserters', such as Kamenev and Zinoviev, who advised against a Bolshevik coup until the Party was stronger. Later, in the post-Lenin power struggle, he would use the record of their lack of resolution in October 1917 as a weapon against them.

During the period of crisis and civil war that accompanied the efforts of the Bolsheviks to consolidate their authority after 1917, Stalin's non-Russian background proved invaluable. His knowledge of the minority peoples of the old Russian Empire led to his being appointed Commissar (Minister) for Nationalities. In this capacity he became the Bolshevik organiser for the whole of the Caucasus region during the Civil War from 1918 to 1921. The position entitled him to exercise military authority, and this led to a number of disputes with Trotsky, the Bolshevik Commissar for War. Superficially the quarrels were to do with the problem of implementing central orders in local conditions, but at a deeper level they were evidence of a clash of wills. This proved to be the beginning of the well-known personal rivalry between Stalin and Trotsky.

Ironically it was in his role as Commissar for Nationalities that Stalin, the 'wonderful Georgian', first aroused Lenin's distrust. Despite his earlier commitment to Georgian independence, Stalin proved heavy-handed and arrogant in his dismissive treatment of the Georgian national representatives and Lenin was obliged to intervene personally to resolve the situation. Lenin had further cause to complain when he learned from his wife, Krupskaya, that Stalin had treated her with considerable discourtesy. Lenin expressed his criticism of Stalin's behaviour in a written statement that became known as 'Lenin's Testament'. In this document Lenin warned that Stalin, since becoming General Secretary of the Party in 1922, had concentrated too much power in his hands. He went on to propose that Stalin be removed from this position. This did not happen. Lenin was too greatly incapacitated during the last year of his life to be politically active. At his death in January 1924, he had still not taken any formal steps to remove Stalin, and the 'Testament' had not been made public.

2 The Roots of Stalin's Power

However much Lenin may have wished to prevent Stalin from succeeding him as leader, it can be seen with hindsight that the basis of Stalin's power had been laid even before Lenin's death. Lenin and the Party had, unintentionally, already provided Stalin with the means of assuming control. To understand how this had happened we need to appreciate the nature of Soviet government as it had developed after 1917.

When Lenin and the Bolsheviks took power in 1917 they were untrained in the skills of government. All their previous efforts had been directed towards preparing for revolution. They had not planned a detailed programme for governing Russia and had to learn the job as they went along. Governments in most countries could call upon tradition and precedent to guide them. A revolutionary government had no such guide-lines; the procedures to be followed were uncertain. This created opportunities for individual advancement which, in more stable times, would not have existed. It is arguable that in a traditional system of government, with a clearly defined pattern of promotion, Stalin would have made little progress. His attempts to rise would have been fully visible and, therefore, preventable. However, Soviet Russia in 1924 was not a traditional system of government. Lenin had given no clear indication what the power-structure should be after he had gone. In the uncertain atmosphere that followed his death a number of pieces of luck helped Stalin to promote his own claims; it was very much a matter of being in the right place at the right time. However, it would be wrong to ascribe his success wholly to good fortune. The luck had to be used. Stalin may have lacked brilliance, but he did not lack ability. His particular qualities of dogged perseverance and willingness to

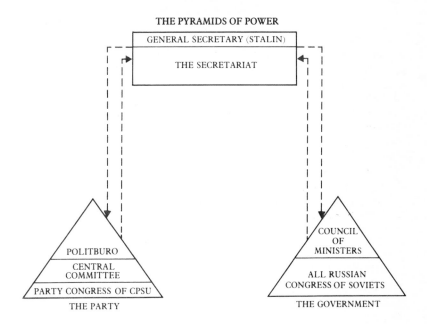

undertake laborious administrative tasks were ideally suited to the times.

*The government of Soviet Russia as it had developed by 1924 had two main features: the Council of Peoples' Commissars (equivalent to a cabinet of ministers), responsible for creating government policies, and the Secretariat (equivalent to the civil service), responsible for carrying out those policies. Both these bodies were staffed and controlled by the Bolshevik Party. It has to be stressed that the vital characteristic of this governmental system was that the Party ruled. By 1922 all other political parties had been outlawed and Soviet Russia was a one-party state. Membership of that one party was essential for all who held administrative or government posts at whatever level.

The Soviet government was thus the formal expression of the Party's control. In this situation the various conferences, committees and congresses that made up the organisation of Party and government became increasingly important. As government grew in scope certain posts, which initially had not been considered especially significant, began to provide their holders with the levers of power. This had not been the intention, but was the unforeseen result of the emerging pattern of Bolshevik rule. It was in this context that Stalin's previous appointments to key posts in both government and Party were to prove so important. These appointments had been:

People's Commissar for Nationalities (1917)

Liaison Officer between Politburo and Orgburo (1919)

Head of the Workers' and Peasants' Inspectorate (1919)

General Secretary of the Communist (Bolshevik) Party (1922)

As Commissar for Nationalities, Stalin was in charge of the officials in the many regions and republics that made up the USSR (the official title of the Soviet state after 1922). As the official responsible for liaison between the Politburo (the Central Committee's inner cabinet) and the Orgburo (the Party's Bureau of Organisation), Stalin was in a unique position to monitor both the Party's policy and the Party's personnel. As Head of the Workers' Inspectorate, he was entitled to oversee the work of all government departments. As General Secretary, he was the vital link-man with access to the personal files of all Party members. He was responsible for recording and conveying Party policy.

These posts had not been meant to confer power on Stalin. The Politburo, of which he had been a member since 1917, had appointed him simply because of his reputation for hard work and painstaking attention to detail. Indeed, it was about this time that an exiled Menshevik described him as 'a grey blur', and Trotsky referred to him as 'an eminent mediocrity'. Even when he was made General Secretary of the Party there was little excitement. Nobody appeared to see it as a portent of anything significant. Some of his biographers suggest that Stalin himself did not at first realise the full importance of what had happened. Writers such as Edward Crankshaw and Norman Stone argue that Stalin was not a planner who carefully plotted his way to the top but an opportunist who, because of his willingness to seize the moment, found power coming within his grasp. Whatever Stalin's intentions may have been at this stage, it would appear that none of his contemporaries had grasped the full political significance of his possession of these administrative posts.

In effect, Stalin became the indspensable link in the chain of Communist Party and Soviet government command. Above all, what these posts gave him was the power of patronage, the right to appoint individuals to official positions in the Party and government. He used this authority to place his own supporters in key positions. Since they then owed their place to him (he could fire as well as hire), Stalin could count on their support in the voting in the various committees and congresses which made up the organisation of the Soviet Union.

*Such were the levers in Stalin's possession during the Party in-fighting over the succession to Lenin. No other contender came anywhere near matching Stalin in his hold on the Party machine. Whatever the ability of the individuals or groups who opposed him or the strength of their arguments, he could always out-vote and, therefore, out-manoeuvre them.

Stalin's advantages over his rivals had been increased by certain recent changes in the structure of the Communist Party. Between 1923 and 1925 the Party, with the declared aim of increasing the number of true proletarians in its ranks, had undertaken 'the Lenin enrolment'. This resulted in the CPSU increasing in size from about three hundred thousand in 1922 to about six hundred thousand by 1925. The new members were predominantly poorly-educated and politically-unsophisticated, but they had sufficient understanding to appreciate that the many privileges which came with Party membership depended on their being loyal to those who had first admitted them into the Bolshevik ranks. The responsibility for supervising and vetting 'the Lenin enrolment' had fallen largely to the officials in the Secretariat who worked directly under Stalin as General Secretary. In this way, the expansion of the Party added to his growing power of patronage. E. H. Carr describes this as being a change 'from the elite party of Lenin to the mass party of Stalin'. It provided the General Secretary with a reliable body of votes in the various Party committees at local and central level.

Another lasting feature of Lenin's period that proved of great value to Stalin was what had become known as the 'attack upon factionalism'. This referred to Lenin's condemnation of the Party's squabbling which had so irritated him during the Civil War period. What this rejection of 'factionalism' effectively did was to frustrate any serious attempt to criticise Party decisions or policies. Contrary to the tradition of internal debate among Bolsheviks, it became extremely difficult to mount any form of legitimate opposition within the CPSU. Stalin was a beneficiary of this ban on criticism of the Party line. The charge of 'factionalism' provided him with a ready weapon for resisting challenges to the authority he had begun to exercise.

*There was an associated factor that legitimised Stalin's position. Stalin became heir to what has been described as the 'Lenin legacy'. By this is meant the tradition of authority and leadership that Lenin had established during his lifetime, and the veneration in which he was held after his death. It is only a slight exaggeration to say that in the eyes of the Communist Party Lenin became a god; his words, actions and decisions became unchallengeable, and all arguments and disputes within the Party were settled by reference to his prescriptions. Lenin became the measure of the correctness of Soviet theory and practice. Soviet Communism became Leninism. After 1924, if a Party member could assume the mantle of Lenin and appear to carry on Lenin's work, he would establish a formidable claim to power. This is what Stalin began to do.

Here a paradox needs to be explained. In theory the Bolshevik Party was a collective organisation. In accordance with its Marxist principles, it was suspicious of leaders and individuals. It believed that it had the right to wield authority because it represented the will, not of any individual but of the masses (the proletariat). The Party had never elected a leader and not even Lenin had been accorded that title. However, no matter what the theory may have been, the practice proved to be very different. The intensity of the struggle for sheer survival after 1917 had meant that power had shifted increasingly to the centre. Such had been Lenin's moral ascendancy among the Bolsheviks, that he had come to represent the Party itself. The collective principle had in practice been superseded by the leadership principle. There is a case for arguing that this was a return to the Russian tradition of central authority that the Tsars had exercised.

3 Stalin versus Trotsky

After Lenin's death the Politburo (consisting of Rykov, Tomsky, Kamenev, Zinoviev, Trotsky and Stalin) publicly proclaimed their intention to continue as a collective leadership, but behind the scenes the competition for individual authority had already begun. In the manoeuvring, Stalin gained an advantage by being the one to deliver the oration at Lenin's funeral. Appearances matter, and the sight of Stalin as leading mourner suggested a continuity between him and Lenin, an impression heightened by the contents of his speech in which in the name of the Party he humbly dedicated himself to follow in the tradition of the deceased leader:

1 In leaving us, comrade Lenin commended us to hold high and pure the great calling of Party Member. We swear to thee, Comrade Lenin, to honour thy command.
   In leaving us, Comrade Lenin commanded us to keep the unity
5 of our Party as the apple of our eye. We swear to thee, Comrade Lenin, to honour thy command.
   In leaving us, Comrade Lenin ordered us to maintain and strengthen the dictatorship of the proletariat. We swear to thee, Comrade Lenin, to exert our full strength in honouring thy
10 command.
   In leaving us, Comrade Lenin ordered us to strengthen with all our might the union of workers and peasants. We swear to thee, Comrade Lenin, to honour thy command.
   In leaving us, Comrade Lenin ordered us to strengthen and
15 expand the Union of the Republics. We swear to thee, Comrade Lenin, to honour thy command.
   In leaving us, Comrade Lenin enjoined us to be faithful to the Communist International. We swear to thee, Comrade Lenin, that we shall dedicate our lives to the enlargement and reinforce-
20 ment of the union of the workers of the whole world, the Communist International.

*Trotsky was conspicuous by his absence from the funeral. This was one in a list of serious tactical mistakes that Stalin's chief rival made. Trotsky later complained that Stalin had not informed him of the date of the funeral; this may well have been true, but it seemed a very lame excuse and raised doubts about his respect for Lenin's memory. Trotsky's was a complex personality. He was one of those figures in history who may be described as having been their own worst enemy. Despite his many gifts and intellectual brilliance, he had serious weaknesses that undermined his chances of success. At times, he was unreasonably self-assured; at other critical times, he suffered from diffidence and lack of judgement. An example of this had occurred earlier, at the time of Stalin's mishandling of the Georgian question. Lenin's annoyance with Stalin had offered Trotsky a golden opportunity for undermining Stalin's position, but for some unexplained reason Trotsky had declined to attack. Now, in January 1924, he had already allowed Stalin to gain an advantage over him.

What is remarkable about this is that Trotsky, by his own account, was well aware of the danger that Stalin represented. In 1924 he prophesied to Smirnov, one of his own supporters, that Stalin would become 'the dictator of the USSR'. When Smirnov expressed surprise, Trotsky gave a strikingly accurate analysis of the basis of Stalin's power in the Party:

1 He is needed by all of them; by the tired radicals, by the
    bureaucrats, by the Nepmen, the upstarts, by all the worms that
    are crawling out of the upturned soil of the manured revolution.
    He knows how to meet them on their own ground, he speaks their
5 language and he knows how to lead them. He has the deserved
    reputation of an old revolutionary. He has will and daring. Right
    now he is organising around himself the sneaks of the Party, the
    artful dodgers.

*At this juncture an obvious hurdle in Stalin's way was Lenin's 'Testament'. If it were to be published it would discredit his claim to have been Lenin's loyal lieutenant. However, here, as so often during this period, fortune favoured him. Had the document been made public, not only would the strictures on Stalin have been revealed, but also those on Trotsky, Zinoviev and Kamenev. Nearly all the members of the Politburo had reason for suppressing the 'Testament'. This is evident from its contents:

1 **25th December 1922**
    Since he became General Secretary, Comrade Stalin has concen-
    trated in his hands immeasurable power, and I am not sure that
    he will always know how to use that power with sufficient

5 caution. On the other hand Comrade Trotsky, as has been shown
already by his struggle against the Central Committee over the
question of the People's Commissariat of Means of Communica-
tion, is distinguished not only by his outstanding qualities
(personally he is the most capable man in the present Central
10 Committee) but also by his excess of self-confidence and a
readiness to be carried away by the purely administrative side of
affairs.

The qualities of these two outstanding leaders of the present
Central Committee might lead quite accidentally to a split, and if
15 our Party does not take steps to prevent it the split might arise
unexpectedly. I shall not try to describe any other members of the
Central Committee according to their personal qualities. I will
simply remind you that the October episode involving Zinoviev
and Kamenev was not, of course, accidental but that it ought not
20 to be used seriously against them, any more than the non-
Bolshevism of Trotsky.

Of the younger members of the Central Committee I would like
to say a few words about Bukharin. Bukharin is not only the most
valuable and the most able theorist in the Party but may
25 legitimately be considered the favourite of the whole Party. But
his theoretical views can only with the greatest hesitation be
regarded as fully Marxist.

Postscript, 4th January 1923

Stalin is too rude, and this fault, entirely supportable in relations
30 amongst us Communists, becomes insupportable in the office of
General Secretary. Therefore, I propose to the comrades to find a
way of removing Stalin from that position and to appoint another
man who in all respects differs from Stalin only in superiority;
namely, more patient, more loyal, more polite, less capricious,
35 and more attentive to comrades.

*When the Central Committee were presented with this document in
May 1924, they realised that it was too damning generally to be used
exclusively against any one individual. They agreed to its being shelved
indefinitely. Trotsky, for obvious personal reasons, went along with the
decision, but in doing so he was throwing away yet another opportunity
to challenge Stalin's right to power. In fact it was Trotsky, not Stalin,
whom the Politburo regarded as the greater danger. With the intention
of blocking Trotsky, Kamenev and Zinoviev joined Stalin in an
unofficial triumvirate within the Politburo. They used Trotsky's
unpopularity with large sections of the Party to isolate him. In this
respect the 'Lenin enrolment' was of considerable assistance to them.
The new proletarian members were hardly the type of men to be
impressed by the cultured image of Trotsky. The seemingly down-to-

earth Stalin was much more to their liking.

The prevailing view of Party members towards Trotsky is an important part of any explanation of Trotsky's political failure and Stalin's success. Because Trotsky was flamboyant and brilliant, while Stalin was unspectacular and methodical, colleagues tended to regard the former as dangerously ambitious and the latter as reliably self-effacing. Trotsky's was the type of personality that attracted either admiration or suspicion, but seldom loyalty. That was why he lacked a genuine following. It is true that he was highly regarded by the Red Army, whose creator he had been, but this was never matched by any comparable political support in the Party. This resulted in Trotsky's invariably having the appearance of an outsider. Adding to his difficulties in this regard was the question-mark against Trotsky's commitment to Bolshevism. Until 1917, as Lenin had noted in his 'Testament', Trotsky had been a Menshevik. This led to the suspicion that his conversion had been a matter of expediency rather than conviction. Many of the old-guard Bolsheviks regarded Trotsky as a Menshevik upstart.

Such views were to dog him when, having overcome his initial loss of nerve, he tried to take the attack to his opponents. Trotsky bitterly condemned the growth of bureaucracy in the Party and appealed for a return to 'Party democracy'. He pressed his views in the annual Party Congresses and in the meetings of the Central Committee and the Politburo. He expanded his arguments in a series of essays, the most controversial of which was *Lessons of October*, in which he criticised Kamenev and Zinoviev for their past disagreements with Lenin. The assault was ill-judged, since it invited retaliation in kind. Trotsky's Menshevism and his own frequent divergences from Lenin were highlighted in a number of books and pamphlets, most notably Kamenev's, *Lenin or Trotsky*.

*Stalin could stand back and observe his rivals destroying each other. Bearing in mind his later extremism, it is an extraordinary fact that at this time Stalin was able to play the role of the great moderate who refused to become embroiled in Party warfare. Even Trotsky's censures on bureaucracy, which were obviously aimed principally at him, left Stalin largely unscathed. What Trotsky meant by bureaucracy was the abandonment of democratic discussion in the Party and the growth in the centralised power of the Secretariat, which was able to make decisions and operate policies without reference to ordinary Party members. Trotsky complained that officials were becoming the masters, rather than the servants, of the Party. In trying to expose Stalin's bureaucratic tendencies, Trotsky overlooked the essential fact that Bolshevik rule since 1917 had always been a bureaucracy. It might have been called other names, like Secretariat and *apparat*, and its officials might have been known by good revolutionary terms like *cadres*, but it was a bureaucracy all the same. Therefore, Trotsky was going against what Lenin had sanctioned and Stalin had continued. After all, it was because the Soviet state functioned as a bureaucracy that Party members received privileges in political and public life. Trotsky was hardly likely to gain significant support from the Party on this issue, as members had a vested interest in bureaucracy.

With Trotsky worsted in the dispute and forced temporarily to retreat, Stalin was free to take the initiative. His open attack on Trotsky and other rivals centred on two fundamental issues in the politics of the Soviet Union in the 1920s. These were the NEP and 'Socialism in one Country'. The issues overlap but it makes for clarity of understanding if they are considered separately.

a) NEP

The New Economic Policy went back to 1921. At the Party Congress of 1921 Lenin had persuaded his fellow Bolsheviks to accept the NEP, in an attempt to lessen the famine that had afflicted large parts of Russia since 1918. Essentially, this was a relaxation of the severe economic controls (known as War Communism) enforced by the government during the Civil War. Under the NEP the peasants were allowed to sell their surplus produce for profit, traditional markets were permitted and money was allowed to be used again. These concessions were a departure from hard-line socialism. Lenin admitted this but said, 'let the peasants have their little bit of capitalism as long as we retain the power'. Lenin had visualised the NEP as a temporary measure but, since it fulfilled its chief objective of providing enough food for the Russian population, it was retained as the official Bolshevik policy towards the peasantry.

At the time of Lenin's death the question was already being asked as to whether the NEP was to last indefinitely. The Party members who were unhappy with it saw its retention as a betrayal of revolutionary principle. They objected to the preferential treatment towards the peasantry which the Policy entailed; the peasants, they argued, were being allowed to slow the pace of Soviet Russia's advance to a truly proletarian state, which had been the whole object of the 1917 Revolution. Those members critical of the NEP were broadly referred to as Left Communists. Those who accepted that as long as the NEP continued to meet the nation's food needs it should be preserved came under the general heading of Right Communists.

It is important not to exaggerate the difference of principle between Left and Right. Although fierce disputes were to arise over the issue, initially the disagreement was simply about timing: how long should the NEP be allowed to run? However, in the power struggle of the 1920s these superficial differences were deepened into questions of political orthodoxy and Party loyalty. A rival's attitude towards the

NEP might be a weakness to be exploited; if it could be established that his views indicated deviant Marxist thinking it became possible to undermine, if not destroy, his position in the Party.

b) Socialism in One Country

Closely related to the NEP debate was the question of how the Soviet Union should plan for the future. This would have been a demanding issue whether or not there had been a power struggle. What the rivalry for leadership did was to intensify the argument. The USSR was a poor country. If it was to modernise and overcome its poverty it would have to industrialise. All recent history had shown that a strong industrial base was an absolute essential for a modern state and there was little disagreement among Soviet Communists about that. The quarrel was not over whether the USSR should industrialise, but over the means and speed of achieving it.

At the time of the October Revolution, Russia had a predominantly agricultural economy. Eighty per cent of the population were peasants. The irony was that the proletarian revolution had occurred in a country without a proletariat. It was very difficult to make October 1917 fit the classic Marxist model of a workers' revolution. Lenin had been very conscious of this and had decided that the link between the Party and the peasants must be maintained for the foreseeable future.

The industrial expansion that had taken place in the previous century, in such countries as Germany and Britain, had relied on the availability of capital (money for investment) and on a ready supply of exploitable natural and human resources. Russia had plentiful resources, but these were at a low level of exploitation, and it certainly did not possess significant amounts of capital. Nor could it borrow any; after 1917 Bolshevik Russia's ideology explicitly rejected capitalist methods of finance. Even had the ideology not forbidden it, there were few countries after 1917 willing to risk the dangers of investing in revolutionary Russia. The only resource, therefore, was the Russian people themselves. If the Soviet Union was to industrialise it would have to be done by persuading or forcing the peasant population to produce a food surplus that could then be sold abroad to raise capital for industrial investment. Both Left and Right agreed that this was the only solution, but, whereas the Right were content to rely on persuasion, the Left demanded that the conservative peasantry be coerced into line.

*It was Trotsky who most clearly represented the view of the Left on this. However, for him the industrialisation debate was secondary to the far more demanding question of Soviet Russia's role as the organiser of international revolution. What inspired Trotsky's politics was his belief in 'Permanent Revolution'. He interpreted the events in Russia since 1917 simply as a prelude to proletarian revolution worldwide. If it came to a choice, the interests of the USSR would have to be subordinated to the greater cause of international revolution. Trotsky asserted that true revolutionary socialism could be achieved in the USSR only if there occurred a genuinely international uprising. The Soviet Union, he believed, could not stand alone. With its vast peasant population and undeveloped proletariat, Russia would prove 'incapable of holding her own against conservative Europe'. Therefore, he contended that the immediate task of the CPSU was not to concern itself with the internal needs of the Soviet Union but 'to export revolution'. This was very much the voice of international Menshevism, Trotsky's old party. Once again he had given his adversaries a weapon to turn against him.

Stalin countered Trotsky's concept of 'Permanent Revolution' with his own slogan of 'Socialism in One Country'. What this term conveyed was that the USSR, by its own unaided efforts, would solve its present agricultural and industrial problems, and would build a modern state, the equal of any nation in the world. Under this banner, Stalin was able to characterise Trotsky as an enemy of the Soviet Union. Trotsky's ideas were condemned as an affront to Lenin and the Bolshevik Revolution. An image was created of Trotsky as an isolated figure, a posturing, Jewish, intellectual, whose abstractions about international revolution threatened the security of the Soviet Union. Trotsky's position was further weakened by the fact that throughout the 1920s there was in the Soviet Union an ever-present fear of imminent invasion by the combined capitalist nations. Although this fear was ill-founded, the tense atmosphere it created made Trotsky's notion of the USSR's engaging in foreign revolutionary wars appear even more irresponsible. A number of historians, including E. H. Carr and Isaac Deutscher, have remarked on Stalin's ability to rally support and silence opponents at critical moments by taking on the role of the great Russian patriot intent on saving the nation from its internal and external enemies.

4 The Defeat of Trotsky and the Left

Trotsky's defeats in the propaganda war of the 1920s meant that he was in no position to persuade either the Politburo or the Central Committee to vote in sufficient numbers in favour of his proposals. Stalin's ability 'to deliver the votes' in the crucial divisions was decisive. Following a vote against him in the 1925 Party Congress, Trotsky was relieved of his position as Commissar for War. Instrumental in packing Congress against him were Kamenev and Zinoviev, the respective Chairmen of the Moscow and Leningrad Soviets. They used their influence over the local Party organisations to ensure that it was a pro-Stalin, anti-Trotsky, Congress that gathered.

Kamenev and Zinoviev had been Stalin's chief agents in the task of undermining Trotsky. They had been motivated by a personal dislike of Trotsky, who had sought to embarrass them be reminding the Party of their failure to support Lenin in 1917. Now it was their turn to be ousted. Doubtless, with Trotsky already weakened, Stalin's thoughts had already turned to the problem of how to deal with these two key figures, who were now his potential rivals. In the event, they created a trap for themselves. In 1925 Kamenev and Zinoviev, worried by the USSR's economic backwardness, publicly stated that it would require the victory of proletarian revolution in the capitalist nations in order for the Soviet Union to achieve socialism. Zinoviev wrote: 'When the time comes for the revolution in other countries and the proletariat comes to our aid, then we shall again go over to the offensive. For the time being we have only a little breathing space.' He called for an end to the NEP, restrictions on the peasants, and enforced industrialisation. It was understandable that Kamenev and Zinoviev, party bosses in the Soviet Union's only genuinely industrial areas, Moscow and Leningrad, should have thought in these terms.

*Their viewpoint formed the basis of what was termed the 'New Opposition' (or 'United Opposition'), but it appeared to be indistinguishable from Trotskyism. It was no surprise, therefore, when Trotsky joined his former opponents in 1926 to form a 'Trotskyite–Kamenevite–Zinovievite' opposition bloc. Again, Stalin's control of the Party machine was his greatest asset. The Party Congress declined to be influenced by pressure from the 'New Opposition'. Stalin's supporters among the Right Communists (chiefly Bukharin, Rykov and Tomsky) combined to outvote the bloc. Kamenev and Zinoviev were dismissed from their posts as Soviet Chairmen, to be replaced by two of Stalin's staunchest allies, Molotov in Moscow and Kirov in Leningrad. Soon afterwards, Trotsky was expelled from both the Politburo and the Central Committee.

Trotsky would still not admit defeat. In 1927, on the tenth anniversary of the Bolshevik rising, he tried to rally support in a direct challenge to Stalin's authority. Even fewer members of Congress than before were prepared to side with him and he was again outvoted. His complete failure led to the Congress accepting Stalin's proposal that Trotsky be expelled from the Party altogether. An internal exile order against him in 1927 was followed two years later by total exile from the USSR.

*In the last analysis, Stalin's victory over Trotsky was not a question of ability or principle. Stalin won because Trotsky lacked a power base. Trotsky's superiority as a speaker and writer, and his greater intellectual gifts, counted for little when set against Stalin's control of the Party machine. It is difficult to see how after 1924 Trotsky could have ever mounted a serious challenge to his rival. Even had his own particular failings not inhibited him from action at vital moments, Trotsky never possessed sufficient understanding, let alone control, of the political system as it operated in Soviet Russia. Politics is the art of the possible. After 1924 all the possibilities belonged to Stalin.

5 The Defeat of the Right

Although Stalin's victory over the Right Opposition is best studied as a feature of his industrialisation programme, it is important also to see it as the last stage in the consolidation of his authority over the Party and the Soviet Union. The defeat of the Right marks the end of any serious attempt to limit his power. From the late 1920s to his death in 1953 he would become increasingly dictatorial.

The major representatives of the Right were Rykov, the Chairman of the Central Committee, Tomsky, the leader of the trade unions, and Bukharin, the editor of *Pravda* and the outstanding economic theorist in the Party. It had been these three who had served Stalin ably and loyally in his outmanoeuvring of Trotsky and the Left. Politically the Right were by no means as challenging to Stalin as the Trotskyite bloc had been. What made Stalin move against them was that they stood in the way of the industrial and agricultural schemes that he began to implement in 1928.

Historians are uncertain precisely when Stalin decided that the answer to the Soviet Union's growth problem was the imposition of collectivisation and industrialisation. It is unlikely to have been an early decision; the probability is that it was another piece of opportunism. Having defeated the Left politically he may then have felt free to adopt their economic policies. This would not have been mere perversity. Stalin had never fully committed himself on economic matters. His stance as a moderate had served its purpose in depicting his opponents as extremists. Perhaps he now considered that he was in a position to judge policies on their economic merits, rather than as counters in the power game. Some scholars have recently suggested that in 1928 Stalin became genuinely concerned at the serious grain shortage and decided that the only way to avoid a crisis was to resort to the drastic methods of collectivisation. It no longer mattered that this had been the very solution that the Left had advanced as they were now out of the way.

For some time it had been the view of Bukharin and the Right that an artificial speeding-up of industrialisation in the USSR was unnecessary. They argued that it would be more productive, and less disruptive, to let industry grow naturally. The State should assist, but it should not direct. Similarly, the peasants should not be controlled and oppressed; this would make them resentful and less productive. The Right agreed that it was from land that the means of financing industrialisation would have to come, but they stressed that, by offering the peasants the chance to become prosperous, far more grain would be produced for sale abroad. Bukharin argued in the Politburo and at the Party

Congress in 1928 that Stalin's aggressive policy of State grain procurements (enforced collections of fixed quotas) from the peasants was counter-productive. He urged that there were economically viable alternatives to these repressive policies. Bukharin was prepared to declare openly what everybody knew, but was afraid to admit, that Stalin's programme was no different from the one that Trotsky had previously advocated.

*The Right suffered from two fundamental weaknesses, one ideological, the other organisational. Their economic arguments were not unsound, but in the war-scare atmosphere of the late 1920s they appeared timid and unrealistic. The plea for a soft line with the peasants did not accord with the Party's needs. The times were perceived as requiring a dedicated resistance to the enemies of Revolution both within the USSR and outside. Stalin was able to suggest that the Right were guilty of underestimating the crisis facing the Party and the Soviet Union. He argued that it was a time for closing the ranks in keeping with the tradition of 1917. Here he showed a shrewd understanding of the mentality of Party members. The majority were far more likely to respond to the call for a return to a hard-line policy, such as had helped them survive the desperate days of the Civil War, than they were to risk the Revolution itself by untimely concessions to a peasantry that had no real place in the proletarian future. The Party of Marx and Lenin would not be well served by the policies of the Right.

The difficulty experienced by the Right in trying to make themselves ideologically credible was associated with a problem that had also rendered the Left ineffective. How could they impress their views upon the Party while Stalin remained master of the Party's organisation? The answer was that they could not. A factor which inhibited Bukharin and his colleagues was that they wanted to remain good Party men and it was this sense of loyalty that weakened them in their attempts to oppose Stalin. Fearful of creating 'factionalism', they hoped that they could persuade the whole Party to their way of thinking without causing deep divisions. On occasion they were sharply out-spoken, Bukharin particularly so, but their basic approach was conciliatory. This played into Stalin's hands. Since it was largely his supporters who were responsible for drafting and distributing Party information, it was not difficult for Stalin to portray the Right as an irresponsible and dangerous clique.

*The Right Opposition's only semblance of a power-base from which it could attempt to influence the formation of Party policy lay in the trade unions, whose Central Council was chaired by Tomsky, and in the CPSU's Moscow branch where Uglanov, an admirer of Bukharin, was the leader. When Stalin realised that these might be a source of difficulty he acted quickly and decisively. He sent the ruthless and ambitious young Politburo member, Kaganovich, to undertake a purge of the suspect trade unionists; the Right proved totally incapable of organising resistance to this political *blitzkrieg*. Molotov, Stalin's faithful henchman, was dispatched to Moscow where he enlisted the support of the pro-Stalin members to effect a similar purge of the local Party officials.

By early 1929 Tomsky was no longer the national trade union leader; Uglanov had been replaced in the Moscow Party organisation; Rykov had been superseded as premier by Molotov, and Bukharin had been voted out as Chairman of the Comintern and had lost his place in the Politburo. Tomsky, Rykov and Bukharin, the main trio of the 'Right Opportunists' as they were termed by the Stalinist press, were allowed to remain in the Party but only after they had publicly admitted the error of their ways. Stalin's triumph over both Left and Right was complete. The grey blur was on the way to becoming the Red Tsar.

Making Notes on 'Stalin: The Rise to Power'

Your notes should help you to understand Stalin's early career as a Bolshevik revolutionary, but your chief task is to provide yourself with a record of the reasons for Stalin's rise to power in the USSR. The following headings and questions should prove useful:

1 **Background:** What led Stalin to become a revolutionary? In what ways were his Georgian origins important?
2 **The Roots of Stalin's Power:** Why was Stalin in such a strong position in 1924 to begin his bid for power? How did Lenin's legacy help him? How was he aided by the structure of Soviet government?
3 **Stalin v Trotsky:** What were Stalin's personal and political strengths? What were Trotsky's weaknesses? Why was Trotsky never in a position to challenge Stalin effectively?
   a) **NEP:** How would you distinguish between Left and Right attitudes towards NEP? Why was NEP such a key issue?
   b) **Socialism in One Country:** What were the essential differences between 'Socialism in One Country' and 'Permanent Revolution' as responses to Soviet Russia's needs in the 1920s?
4 **The Defeat of Trotsky and the Left:** How did Stalin out-manoeuvre Trotsky? What was meant by the 'New Left' and why did it fail in its challenge to Stalin?
5 **The Defeat of the Right:** Who were the Right? What viewpoint did they represent? Why were they no more successful against Stalin than the Left?

Answering essay questions on 'Stalin: The Rise to Power'

It is unlikely that you will ever be asked for a narrative of the years

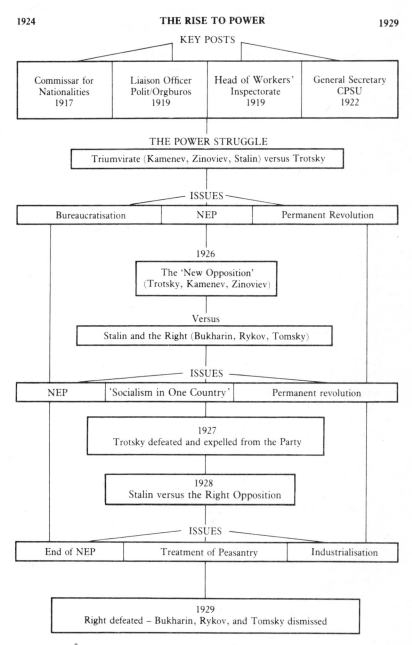

Summary – Stalin: the Rise to Power, 1924–29

1924–29. However it is vital, nonetheless, that you have a firm knowledge of the political developments of that period. A grasp of how Stalin came to power is basic to an understanding of the rest of this book. Do bear in mind that there is an important connection between the power struggle described in this chapter, the economic issues covered in Chapter 3, and the foreign policy analysed in Chapter 5.

The power struggle of the 1920s is a favourite topic among examiners. Their questions break down into three main categories:
1 The roots of Stalin's authority.
2 His defeat of Trotsky and the Left.
3 His defeat of Bukharin and the Right.

Typical questions on these themes are:
a) Discuss the view that 'Stalin already held the reins of power at the time of Lenin's death in 1924'.
b) Why was it Stalin and not Trotsky who emerged as the leader of the USSR by 1929?
c) Explain why the Right Bolsheviks were unable to mount an effective challenge to Stalin in the power struggle of the 1920s.

Make a list of the issues involved in the power struggle and then put them in order of importance. It would help clarify your thoughts if you were to add the reasons for your choice. With this list to guide you, construct an essay plan for the question b). You will find it useful to refer back to the essay plan in the study guide at the end of Chapter 1. Stress Stalin's strengths and Trotsky's weaknesses and relate these to the power structure in the USSR. Note that the question is as much about Trotsky as it is about Stalin. The balance of your answer should reflect this.

Source based questions on 'Stalin: The Rise to Power'

1 Lenin's 'Testament'
Read the extracts from Lenin's letter on pages 15–16, and then answer the following questions:
a) What individual reservations does Lenin have about Stalin, Trotsky, Zinoviev and Kamenev, and Bukharin?
b) What was Lenin's aim in making these observations?
c) In what ways do the contents of this document suggest that it was unlikely to be published after Lenin's death?

2 Stalin's Speech at Lenin's Funeral
Read the extracts from Stalin's speech on page 14, and from Trotsky's

analysis on page 15, and then answer the following questions:

a) What promises does Stalin make in regard to Party unity?

b) What commitments does Stalin make regarding future Soviet domestic and foreign policy?

c) What would you judge Stalin's purpose to be in his constant repetition of Lenin's name?

d) How useful is this document as evidence of Stalin's wish to suggest a continuity between himself and Lenin?

e) How far do Trotsky's observations to Smirnov suggest that Stalin had struck the right note with Party members with his funeral speech?

CHAPTER 3

Stalin and the Soviet Economy

1 Background

Stalin's economic policy had one essential aim, the modernisation of the Soviet Union, and two essential methods, collectivisation and industrialisation. The collectivisation of agriculture, which substituted State ownership of the land for individual peasant-proprietorship, was a means to an end. It was intended to serve the needs of the industrialisation drive, which began with the introduction of the first Five-Year Plan (FYP) (1928–32). In 1929 Stalin defined collectivisation as 'the setting up of *kolkhozy* [collective farms] and *sovkhozy* [state farms] in order to squeeze out all capitalist elements from the land'. The *kolkhozy* were to be run as co-operatives in which the peasants would pool their resources and share the labour and the wages; the *sovkhozy* were to contain peasants working directly for the State, which would pay them a wage. In practice there were only minor differences between these two types of farm. Both were to be the means by which private peasant-ownership was ended and agriculture was made to serve the interests of the Soviet State. The plan was to group between 50 and 100 holdings into one unit. The reasoning was that large farms would be efficient and would allow the effective use of agricultural machinery; the motorised tractor became the outstanding symbol of this proposed mechanisation of Soviet farming. In addition to increasing the supply of cheap food for home consumption and sale abroad, efficient farming would decrease the number of rural workers needed and thus release workers for the new factories.

*In 1926 the justification for Stalin's crash programme of collectivisation and industrialisation had been provided by the momentous decision of the Party Congress of that year to undertake 'the transformation of our country from an agrarian into an industrial one, capable by its own efforts of producing the necessary means'. Stalin was to turn that resolution into reality. The Revolution in 1917 had succeeded in placing the Bolsheviks in power, but had not determined what their future policies should be; hence the arguments over the NEP, 'Permanent Revolution' and 'Socialism in One Country'. What Stalin's massive restructuring of agriculture and industry did was to clarify the situation. From 1928 onwards, with the introduction of collectivisation and industrialisation, there were no doubts concerning the Soviet Union's economic strategies and objectives. The Soviet State would centralise and control the nation's economy. This momentous decision is often referred to by historians as 'the second Revolution'.

It is also frequently defined as 'revolution from above'. To understand the implications of this description it is necessary to put Stalin's industrialisation drive in the context of Marxist ideology. In his analysis of the class war, Karl Marx had maintained that a society's political and social system was a direct product of its economic structure; it was on its economic base that its political and institutional super-structure rested. In theory, 1917 had been a revolution from below. The Bolshevik-led proletariat had broken the remnants of old-style Tsarist oppression and had begun to construct a state in which the workers ruled. Bukharin and the Right had used this interpretation to argue that, since the USSR was now a proletarian-based society, the economy should be left to develop at its own pace, without interference from the government. In marked contrast, Stalin's economic programme from the late 1920s onwards proposed the inversion of this process. He stood Marxist theory on its head. Instead of the economy determining the character of the political system, the political system would determine the character of the economy.

*This is not to suggest that the centralising of economic planning under Stalin was entirely novel. In Lenin's time the central planning agency, *Gosplan*, had been introduced. However what was different about Stalin's plans was their scale, speed and intensity. Under Stalin, State control was to be comprehensive and all-embracing. Historians are still not entirely sure of Stalin's motivation. He had no great reputation as an economic thinker before 1928 and seems to have relied heavily on the theories of Preobrazhensky, the leading economist among the Left Bolsheviks. Perhaps the strongest probability is that Stalin saw a hard-line policy as providing the means of consolidating his political authority over Party and government. As was seen in Chapter 2, it is not possible entirely to separate political and economic considerations when studying the power struggle of the 1920s. It is also noteworthy that when he introduced his radical economic changes Stalin proclaimed that they marked as significant a stage in Soviet Communism as had Lenin's fateful decision to sanction the October rising in 1917. This comparison was obviously intended to enhance his own status as a revolutionary leader following in the footsteps of Lenin. However, it would be wrong to regard Stalin's policy as wholly a matter of political expediency. Judging from his speeches and actions after 1928, he had become convinced that the needs of Soviet Russia could be met only by the collectivisation and industrialisation programme that he initiated. That was the essence of his slogan, 'Socialism in One Country'. The survival of the Revolution and of Soviet Russia depended on the nation's ability to turn itself into a modern industrial society within the shortest possible time. Stalin expressed this with particular clarity in 1931 when he sought to justify the speed of the social transformation that was being brought about by collectivisation and industrialisation:

1 It is sometimes asked whether it is not possible to slow down the

tempo somewhat, to put a check on the movement. No, comrades, it is not possible! The tempo must not be reduced! On the
contrary we must increase it as much as is within our powers and
5 possibilities. This is dictated to us by our obligations to the
working class of the whole world. To slacken the tempo would
mean falling behind. And those who fall behind get beaten. But
we do not want to be beaten. No, we refuse to be beaten! One
feature of old Russia was the continual beatings she suffered
10 because of her backwardness. She was beaten by the Mongol
khans. She was beaten by the Turkish *beys*. She was beaten by the
Polish and Lithuanian gentry. She was beaten by the British and
French capitalists. She was beaten by the Japanese barons. All
beat her – because of her backwardness, military backwardness,
15 cultural backwardness, political backwardness, industrial backwardness, agricultural backwardness. They beat her because to
do so was profitable and could be done with impunity. Do you
remember the words of the pre-revolutionary poet: 'You are poor
and abundant, mighty and powerless, Mother Russia'. Those
20 gentlemen were quite familiar with the verses of the old poet.
They beat her, saying 'You are abundant, so one can enrich
oneself at your expense'. They beat her, saying 'You are poor and
powerless, so you can be beaten and plundered with impunity'.
Such is the law of the exploiters – to beat the backward and weak.
25 It is the jungle law of capitalism. You are backward, you are weak
– therefore you are wrong; hence you can be beaten and enslaved.
You are mighty – therefore you are right; hence we must be wary
of you. That is why we must no longer lag behind.
  We are fifty or a hundred years behind the advanced countries.
30 We must make good this distance in ten years. Either we do it, or
we shall be crushed. This is what our obligations to the workers
and peasants of the USSR dictate to us.

This impassioned appeal to Russian history subordinates all other
considerations to the one driving need of national survival. It was by
reference to this appeal that Stalin would later justify the severity of the
imposed collectivisation of Russian agriculture.

2 Collectivisation

At its introduction in 1928, collectivisation was referred to as 'volun-
tary'. Stalin claimed that it was the free choice of the peasants, but in
practice it was enforced on a very reluctant peasantry. In effect, Stalin
had adopted the ideas of the extreme Left. He justified collectivisation
by playing on the natural antipathy of the Bolsheviks towards the
peasants. In a major propaganda offensive, he identified a class of
'Kulaks', who were holding back the workers' revolution. These

Kulaks were defined as rich peasants who had grown wealthy under the NEP. They monopolised the best land and employed cheap peasant labour to farm it. By hoarding their farm produce and maintaining artificially high food prices, they were exploiting the needs of the workers and poorer peasants to make themselves increasingly prosperous. Unless they were broken as a class, they would prevent the modernisation of the USSR.

However, the concept of a Kulak class has been shown by scholars to have been a Stalinist myth. The so-called Kulaks were really only those industrious peasants who, by their own efforts, had proved somewhat more efficient farmers than their neighbours. In no sense did they constitute the class of exploiting land-owners described in Stalin's propaganda campaign against them. Nonetheless, given the tradition of landlord oppression going back to Tsarist times, the myth of a Kulak class proved a very potent one and provided the pretext for the coercion of the peasantry as a whole – middle and poor peasants, as well as Kulaks.

*Stalin justified his measures towards the peasants in terms of Party principles. Bolshevism was a proletarian creed. It taught that the days of the peasantry as a revolutionary social force had passed. The future belonged to the urban workers. October 1917 had been the first stage in the triumph of this proletarian class. Therefore it was perfectly fitting that the peasantry should, in a time of national crisis, become wholly subservient to the demands of industrialisation. That subservience took the form of a simple formula. The USSR needed industrial investment and manpower. The land could provide both. Surplus grain would be sold abroad to raise investment funds for industry; surplus peasants would be recruited into the industrial labour force.

One part of the formula was correct; for generations the Russian countryside had been overpopulated, creating a chronic land shortage. The other part was a gross and deliberate misrepresentation. There was no grain surplus. Indeed, even in the best years of the NEP food production had seldom matched requirements. Yet Stalin insisted that the problem was not a lack of food supplies but their inefficient distribution. He asserted that the apparent food shortages were the result of grain-hoarding by the rich peasants. This argument was then used to explain the pressing need for collectivisation as a way of securing adequate food production and distribution. It also provided a moral justification for the onslaught on the Kulaks, who were condemned as grain-monopolists, exploiters of poor peasants, and enemies of the Soviet nation in its struggle to modernise itself in the face of international, capitalist, hostility. In some regions 'de–Kulakisation' was undertaken with enthusiasm by the poorer peasants, since it provided them with an excuse to settle old scores and to give vent to local jealousies. Land and property were seized from the minority of better-off peasants, and they and their families were physically attacked. Such treatment was often the prelude to arrest and deportation by the official anti-Kulak squads, authorised by Stalin and modelled on the gangs who had persecuted the peasants during the 'Terror' in the Civil War period (1918–20). The OGPU (which had succeeded the Cheka as the State security force, and which would be renamed the NKVD in 1931) was entrusted with the recruitment and organisation of these squads.

To the mass of the peasantry the renewal of terror as a deliberate policy also served as warning of the likely consequences of resisting the State reorganisation of Soviet agriculture. The destruction of the Kulaks was thus an integral part of the whole collectivisation process. As a Soviet official later admitted: 'most Party officers thought that the whole point of de–Kulakisation was its value as an administrative measure, speeding up tempos of collectivisation'.

*In the period between December 1929 and March 1930, nearly 60% of the peasant farms in the USSR were collectivised. As a result, something little short of a civil war broke out in the countryside. Peasants in their millions resisted the attempted collectivisation. Such was the savagery and the degree of suffering that Stalin called a halt, blaming the troubles on over-zealous officials, 'dizzy with success'. Many of the peasants were allowed to return to their original holdings. However, the delay was only temporary; having cleared his own name by blaming the difficulties on incompetent local officials, Stalin restarted collectivisation in a more determined, if somewhat slower, manner. Western analysts tend to treat Soviet statistics with caution, but, with due allowance for marginal inaccuracy, the following data reveal the extraordinary character of collectivisation. The table indicates that by the end of the 1930s virtually the whole of the peasantry had been collectivised.

Percentage of Peasant Holdings Collectivised in the USSR, 1930–41

1930	1931	1932	1933	1934	1935	1936	1941
23.6%	52.7%	61.5%	66.4%	71.4%	83.2%	89.6%	98.0%

*Behind these remarkable figures lies the story of a massive social upheaval. The peasantry was disorientated and alienated. It either would not or could not co-operate in the deliberate destruction of its traditional way of life. The consequences were increasingly tragic. The majority of peasants ate their seed corn and slaughtered their livestock. There were no harvests left to reap or animals to rear. The Soviet authorities responded by still fiercer coercion, but this simply made matters worse: imprisonment, deportation and execution could not replenish the barns or restock the herds. The ignorance of farming techniques among those Party members (called the 'Twenty-five

Thousand' after the number forming the first contingent) who were sent from the towns to restore food production levels, only added to the disruption. By a bitter irony, even as starvation set in, the little grain that was available was being exported as 'surplus' to obtain the foreign capital that industry demanded. By 1932 the situation on the land was catastrophic, as the following figures show. They are Western estimates based on Soviet statistics.

Consumption of Foodstuffs (in kilos per head)

	Bread	Potatoes	Meat & Lard	Butter
1928	250.4	141.1	24.8	1.35
1932	214.6	125.0	11.2	0.7

Comparative Numbers of Livestock

	Horses	Cattle	Pigs	Sheep and goats
1928	33,000,000	70,000,000	26,000,000	146,000,000
1932	15,000,000	34,000,000	9,000,000	42,000,000

These figures refer to the USSR as a whole. In the urban areas there was relatively more food available. Indeed, a major purpose of the grain requisition squads was to maintain adequate supplies to the industrial regions. This meant that the misery in the countryside was proportionally greater, with areas such as the Ukraine and Kazhakstan suffering particularly severely. The devastation experienced by the Kazhaks can be gauged from the fact that in this period they lost nearly ninety per cent of their livestock.

*Starvation, which in many parts of the Soviet Union persisted throughout the 1930s, was at its worst in the years 1932–33, when there occurred what is best described as a national famine. Collectivisation had induced a degree of peasant despair that for a devastating period destroyed the always tenuous stability of Russian agriculture. In large areas of the USSR the uprooted peasantry had simply stopped producing, either as an act of desperate resistance or through sheer inability to adapt to the bewilderingly new and violently enforced regime. Few peasants understood the economic logic, still less the ideological justification, of it all. The cruel fact was that as a subordinate part of a grand industrial design Soviet agriculture had been burdened with a task that it could not fulfil. The result was that for a significant period it ceased in any meaningful sense to function at all. So great was the migration from the rural to the urban areas that a system of internal passports was introduced in an effort to control the flow. Some idea of the horrors can be obtained from the following eye-witness account:

1 Russia today is in the grip of famine. I walked alone through
villages and twelve collective farms. Everywhere was the cry,
'There is no bread; we are dying'. This cry came to me from every
part of Russia. In a train a Communist denied to me that there
5 was a famine. I flung into the spittoon a crust of bread I had been
eating from my own supply. The peasant, my fellow passenger,
fished it out and ravenously ate it. I threw orange peel into the
spittoon. The peasant again grabbed it and devoured it. The
Communist subsided. . . .
10   The government's policy of collectivisation and the peasants'
resistance to it have brought Russia to the worst catastrophe since
the famine of 1921 swept away the population of whole districts.
                 (report by a Reuter correspondent, 29th March 1932)

It was only from such descriptions by Western visitors that news of the
horrendous events in Russia at this time became known. The official
Stalinist line was that there was no famine. In the whole of the
contemporary Soviet press there were only two oblique references to
the famine. This conspiracy of silence was of more than political
significance. As well as protecting the image of Stalin the great planner,
it effectively prevented the introduction of any measures for remedying
the distress. Since the famine was deemed not to exist Soviet Russia
could not publicly take steps to deal with it. For the same reason it
could not appeal, as had been done during the 1921 famine, for
assistance from the outside world. Thus it was that what Isaac
Deutscher, the historian and former-Trotsykist, called 'the first purely
man-made famine in history' went unacknowledged in order to avoid
discredit falling on its perpetrator. Not for the last time, a large
proportion of the Soviet people was sacrificed on the altar of Stalin's
reputation.

   *De-Stalinisation in the 1950s revealed Stalin's crimes against the
Party. However, it was not until the 1980s that Stalin's offences against
the Russian people began to be publicly admitted in the USSR. In the
atmosphere of *glasnost*, associated with the Gorbachev reforms of the
late 1980s, it became possible to say the previously unsayable. In 1989
the Soviet historian, Dmitri Volkogonov, produced the first unexpur-
gated Russian biography of Joseph Stalin. In his book Volkogonov
confirmed many of the suspicions long entertained in the West of
Stalin's inhumanity. Of special interest in relation to the collectivisation
period was Volkogonov's discovery from official Soviet records that
Stalin went into the countryside on only one occasion, in 1928, and
visited a factory only twice.

   Leaving aside humanitarian considerations, it is difficult to justify
collectivisation even on economic grounds. Historians find little evidence to indicate that it provided the Soviet Union with the capital

accumulation anticipated at the time of its introduction. The basic weakness was that there was never a genuine surplus that could be sold to raise capital. Although the famine had eased by 1939, agriculture continued to produce less than was required to feed the Soviet population. Although there was an increase in grain production, stocks of other food stuffs declined. There has been significant speculation among economic analysts that a policy of state taxation of an uncollectivised peasantry would have produced a much higher level of investment capital, while avoiding the social dislocation and misery of Stalin's measures. (This was the very policy that had been urged by Bukharin and the Right.) At a more mundane level it has been observed that if, instead of trying to increase grain production by means of fighting the class war, Stalin and his officials had encouraged the peasants to use effective rat poison and properly ventilated barns the consequent saving of food stocks would have made collectivisation unnecessary. This, of course, is to overlook the ideological dimension of Stalin's land programme and to give no place to his deep sense of vindictiveness towards the Russian peasantry.

Even allowing for the occasional progressive aspect of collectivisation, such as the spread of the MTS (Machine Tractor Stations), the overall picture is unimpressive. By 1939 Soviet agricultural productivity had barely returned to the level recorded for Tsarist Russia in 1913. But the most damning consideration still remains the famine, which, at least in its most excessive forms, was avoidable. Western calculations of the number of Soviet peasants who died as a direct result of the famines of the 1930s vary between ten and fifteen million.

3 Industrialisation

Stalin's programme of industrialisation for the USSR is best understood as an attempt to establish a war economy. He declared that he was promoting a great leap forward, as a war on the inefficiencies of Russia's past, as a war against the class enemies within, and as a preparation for war against the nation's capitalist enemies abroad. The war image also explains the form that Soviet industrialisation took. For Stalin, industry meant heavy industry. He saw iron, steel, and oil production as the genuine measures of industrial growth, as it was these products that provided the sinews of war. He believed that the industrial revolutions of western Europe and North America had been based on iron and steel production. Therefore the USSR would adopt a similar industrial pattern in its drive towards modernisation. The difference would be that, whereas the West had followed the capitalist road, the USSR would take the path of socialism. This was not mere political rhetoric. It has to be remembered that Stalin's industrialisation drive coincided with the period of economic stagnation in the West, known as the Great

Depression. There were grounds for interpreting these current difficulties as evidence of the advent of the final great crisis of Western capitalism, foretold by Marx. Stalin claimed that the USSR was introducing into her own economy the proven technical successes of Western industrialisation but was rejecting totally the self-destructive capitalist system that went with them. By socialist-inspired choice the USSR would avoid the errors that had begun to destroy the Western economies. This gave plausibility to Stalin's concept of a planned economy for the Soviet Union.

*The character of industrialisation under Stalin is best studied in relation to the Five-Year Plans. These were a series of programmes for industrial expansion, expressed in terms of targets of output and production to be reached. Gosplan, the State planning-authority that had been in existence since the early 1920s, was required by Stalin to draw up a list of quotas ranging across the whole of Soviet industry. The process began in 1928 and, allowing for the intervention of the war years 1941–45, lasted until Stalin's death in 1953. There were five separate Plans:

1st FYP – October, 1928 to December, 1932
2nd FYP – January, 1933 to December, 1937
3rd FYP – January, 1938 to June, 1941
4th FYP – January, 1946 to December, 1950
5th FYP – January, 1951 to December, 1955

a) The First Five-Year Plan

The term 'Plan' is misleading. A set of targets is by no means the same thing as a plan. It did not follow that merely because detailed figures were laid down the means of achieving them had been specified. Indeed, real planning was the key element missing from the first FYP. What the statistics represented was a set of ideal targets; in some cases they bore little relation to reality. As with collectivisation, so with industrialisation, local officials and managers tended to launder their production figures in order to give the impression of greater success than had actually been achieved. Precise statistics for the first FYP are, therefore, difficult to determine. A further complication is that three quite distinct versions of the first FYP eventually appeared. Impressed by the apparent progress of the Plan in its early stages, Stalin encouraged the formulation of an 'optimal' plan which reassessed targets upwards. These new quotas were hopelessly unrealistic and stood no chance of being reached. Nonetheless, on the basis of the supposed achievements of this 'optimal' plan the figures were revised still higher. Western analysts suggest the following as the closest approximation to the real figures:

Product (in million tons)	1927–28 1st plan	1932–33 'optimal'	1932 amended	1932 actual
Coal	35.0	75.0	95–105	64.0
Oil	11.7	21.7	40–55	21.4
Iron Ore	6.7	20.2	24–32	12.1
Pig Iron	3.2	10.0	15–16	6.2

*The importance of these figures should not be overestimated. At the time it was the overall design, not the detail, that mattered. Essentially the Plan was a huge propaganda project, aimed at convincing the Soviet people that they were engaged in a great industrial enterprise of their own making. By their own efforts, they were changing the shape and character of the society in which they lived, making it safe from foreign invasion and providing it with the means of achieving greatness. Because of the coercion that was widely used, foreign observers have often lost sight of the idealism that inspired so many of the participants in Soviet Russia's headlong drive for industrialisation. They were not all forced into line. There was, among the young especially, an enthusiasm and a commitment that suggested that many Soviet citizens believed they were genuinely building a new and better society. The term, 'cultural revolution', is an appropriate description of the scale and significance of what was being undertaken under Stalin's leadership. Two renowned Western analysts of Soviet affairs, Alec Nove and Sheila Fitzpatrick, have laid stress on this aspect. They see behind the economic changes of this period a real attempt being made to create a new type of individual, what was called at the time *Homo Sovieticus* (Soviet man), as if a new species had come into being. Stalin told a gathering of Soviet writers that they should regard themselves as 'engineers, directing the reconstruction of the human soul'. The sense of the Soviet people as masters of their own fate comes through in the contemporary slogan, 'There is no fortress that we Bolsheviks cannot storm'. John Scott, an American Communist and one of the many pro-Soviet Western industrial advisers who came to the USSR at this time, described the mixture of idealism and coercion that characterised the early stages of Stalinist industrialisation:

1 Magnitogorsk was a city built from scratch. Within several years, half a billion cubic feet of excavation was done, forty-two million cubic feet of reinforced concrete poured, five million cubic feet of fire bricks laid, a quarter of a million tons of structured steel
5 erected. This was done without sufficient labour, without necessary quantities of the most elementary materials. Brigades of young enthusiasts from every corner of the Soviet Union arrived in the summer of 1930 and did the groundwork of railroad and dam construction necessary. Later, groups of local peasants and

10 herdsmen came to Magnitogorsk because of bad conditions in the villages, due to collectivisation. Many of the peasants were completely unfamiliar with industrial tools and processes. A colony of several hundred foreign engineers and specialists, some of whom made as high as one hundred dollars a day, arrived to
15 advise and direct the work.

From 1928 until 1932 nearly a quarter of a million people came to Magnitogorsk. About three quarters of these new arrivals came of their own free will seeking work, bread-cards, better conditions. The rest came under compulsion.

*It was by such efforts that the first FYP gained its results. After due account has been taken of the falsification of returns at local and national levels, the Plan still remains an extraordinary, if patchy, achievement. Coal, iron, and the generation of electrical power all increased in huge proportions. The production of steel and chemicals (particularly in the key area of fertilisers) was less impressive, while the output of finished textiles actually declined. Not surprisingly, in view of the depredations of collectivisation, village-based handicrafts largely died out. By deliberate design, the production of consumer articles was given a low priority. The harshness of the attitude underlying this decision was further reflected in the reluctance of the Soviet authorities to pay more than passing attention to living conditions in the teeming industrial centres. The supply of accommodation, sub-standard even by the traditionally poor quality of Russian urban housing, failed to meet demand. This neglect of basic social needs was not accidental. It had never been intended that the Plan should be the means of raising living standards. Its purpose was collective, not individual. It called for sacrifice and dedication on the part of the workers in the construction of a socialist state, able to sustain itself economically and militarily in the face of capitalist enmity.

Stalin's stress upon the hostility of the outside world was crucial. It enabled him to brand as national 'sabotage' any resistance to the Plan or failure to achieve its objectives. A series of public trials of industrial 'wreckers', including a number of foreign workers, was used to impress the Party and the masses of the futility of protesting against the rigours of industrialisation. As a prelude to the first FYP, Stalin claimed in 1928 to have discovered an anti-Soviet conspiracy among the mining engineers of Shakhty in the Donbass region. The Shakhty trial was significant as a method of cowing the industrial workforce. It also showed that the privileged position of the skilled workers, the 'bourgeois experts', was to be tolerated no longer.

This attack upon the existing managerial elite was part of a pattern. It relates to the emphasis in the first FYP upon quantity at the expense of quality. The push was towards sheer volume of industrial output, almost as a self-justifying activity that would prove the correctness of

'The Five Year Plan in Four Years'
'Under the Banner of Lenin We Won the Battles for the October Revolution'
'Under the Banner of Lenin We Achieved the Decisive Successes in the Struggle for Socialist Reconstruction'
'Under the Same Banner We Shall Win in the Worldwide Proletarian Revolution'

The Five Year Plan. Poster depicting Stalin as the creator of a powerful industrialized Russia

Stalin's grand economic schemes. Sheila Fitzpatrick has termed this 'gigantomania', the worship of size for its own sake. The quality of the output was not regarded as the measure of success. This may, perhaps, mark a shrewd judgement on Stalin's part. He would have known that the untrained peasants who poured into the new factories, such as those described in John Scott's account, were hardly likely to turn suddenly into skilled workers. It made sense, therefore, at least in the short-term, to shelve the question of efficiency and quality control and to emphasise the economic values of prodigious collective endeavour. Stories circulated regarding machines, factories, and even whole enterprises being ruined because of the workers' ignorance of elementary industrial procedures. These descriptions testified to the problems inherent in basing an industrial revolution on a workforce that in disposition and mentality was essentially rural and conservative.

*Stalin's notions of industrial 'saboteurs' and 'wreckers' allowed him to place the blame for inefficiency and under-production on managers, foremen and operatives who were not prepared to play their proper part in the transformation of Soviet society. OGPU agents and Party *cadres* (political officers) were sent into the factories and onto the construction sites to spy on managers and workers and to report back on their performance.

Once again, political control became the instrument for enforcing economic policy. 'Sabotage' became a blanket term with which to denounce anyone considered to be less than wholly committed to the new Soviet order. The simplest errors, such as being late, accidentally damaging tools, or miscounting items, became a pretext for condemning the unfortunate as being opposed to socialist progress. At a higher level, those overseers or factory managers who proved incapable of fulfilling their production quotas might find themselves on public trial as enemies of the Soviet state. In such an atmosphere, fear and recrimination flourished. Deceit, the doctoring of official returns and inflated output claims became normal practice. Everybody at every level was engaged in a huge game of fraud, pretending that things were other than they were. This was why the Soviet statistics for industrial growth were so unreliable and why it was possible for Stalin to claim in mid-course that the first FYP had already achieved its initial targets and so would become a four year plan. In Stalin's industrial revolution appearances were everything. This was where the logic of 'gigantomania' had led.

*The industrial policies of this time have been described as 'the Stalinist blue-print' or 'Stalin's economic model'. Modern scholars are, however, wary of using such terms. Norman Stone, for example, interprets Stalin's policies not as far-sighted strategy but as 'simply putting one foot in front of the other as he went along'. In no real sense was the first FYP a blue-print or model, if by those words is meant a detailed programme of industrial expansion. Despite the growing tendency in all official Soviet documents of the 1930s to include a fulsome reference to Stalin, the master-planner, there was in fact very little planning, as such, from the top. Broad objectives were declared and heavy emphasis was placed upon certain types of industrial product, but the methods of achieving these targets were left to be worked out by officials and managers on the spot. Stalin's government exhorted, cajoled, and terrorised the workforce into ever greater efforts towards ever greater production, but such planning as there was occurred not at national but at local level. It was the regional and site managers and workers who, struggling desperately to make sense of the instructions they were given from on high, formulated the actual schemes to meet their given production quotas. This was why it was so easy for Stalin and his Kremlin colleagues to accuse lesser officials of inefficiency or sabotage while themselves avoiding any taint of incompetence.

b) The Second and Third Five-Year Plans

The Second FYP (1933–37), begun during the grimmest period of the agricultural famine, was more realistic than the First Plan. Nevertheless, it still revealed the uncoordinated nature of much of the so-called central planning. Over-production occurred in some parts of the economy, under-production in others, with the frequent result that whole branches of industry were held up for lack of essential supplies. The struggle to obtain an adequate supply of materials often led to fierce competition between regions and sectors of industry, all of them anxious to escape the charge of not achieving the goals laid down from above. In consequence, there was considerable unproductive hoarding of resources and a lack of the co-operation necessary for integrated industrial growth. Complaints about poor standards, thinly veiled in order to avoid appearing critical of Stalin and the Plan, continued to be made. The reluctance to expose weaknesses in the Plan had serious repercussions for industrial efficiency. Since no-one was willing to admit that an error in planning or production had taken place, faults went unchecked until they reached proportions that could no longer be hidden. There followed the inevitable search for scape-goats. It was in the period of the Second and Third FYPs that Stalin's political Purges reached their height; in such an all-pervading atmosphere of terror the very charge of 'sabotage' was taken as a proof of guilt. All this had a detrimental effect on productivity. As Alec Nove observes: 'Everywhere there were said to be spies, wreckers, diversionists. There was a grave shortage of qualified personnel, so the deportation of many thousands of engineers and technologists to distant concentration camps represented a severe loss'.

What successes there were occurred again in heavy industry where the Second FYP began to reap the benefit of the creation of large-scale plants under the First Plan. Despite Stalin's statements to the contrary, the living standards of the workers failed to rise. This was due, in part, to the effects of the famine, but also to the continuing neglect in the Plans of consumer goods. Beyond the comfort to be gained from feeling that they were engaged in a great national enterprise, a theme constantly emphasised in the Soviet press, there was little in material terms to help the workers endure the severity of their conditions. Moreover, they were required to accept their lot without complaint. The official line was that all was well.

The Party's control of newspapers, cinema and radio effectively prevented other than a totally favourable view of the Plans and their achievements being presented. A remarkable example of this was the Stakhanovite movement that began in 1935. Allegedly, in August of that year Alexei Stakhanov, a miner, produced in one five-hour shift over fourteen times his required quota of coal. Whatever the truth of the story, his example was seized on by the authorities to indicate what feats were possible in a Soviet Union guided by the great and wise Joseph Stalin. Soviet workers were now to be inspired or shamed into raising their production norms yet higher. Ironically, while many workers did respond positively to the 'Stakhanovite' call for greater output, the fact that they could do so was a sign of how low existing productivity levels had been.

*It is a striking paradox that in a reputedly proletarian state the living standards of the Soviet workers should have been given the lowest place in the order of planning priorities. The explanation has two main aspects: the weakness of the trade unions and the character of the Soviet 'war economy'. Rather than becoming more effective after 1917, the trade union organisations had declined into powerlessness. According to Bolshevik theory, in a truly socialist state such as Russia now was, there was no distinction between the interests of government and those of the workers. Therefore, there was no longer any need for a combative trade union movement. In 1920 Trotsky had taken steps to undermine the position of the unions as independent bodies in the Soviet state. Subsequently, the leadership of the unions had passed into the hands of Party members who became the effective means of enforcing Soviet government requirements upon the workers. In Stalin's industrialisation programme the unions were wholly subservient to the needs of the State. Strikes were not permitted and the traditional demands of workers for better pay and conditions were regarded as selfishly inappropriate in a time of national crisis. A code of 'labour discipline' was drawn up, demanding maximum effort and output; failure to conform could be punished by a range of penalties from loss of wages to imprisonment in forced labour camps. On paper workers' wages improved during the Second FYP, but in real terms, given the continuance of food rationing and high prices, living standards were lower in 1937 than they had been in 1928.

*The sacrifice that all this entailed was justified by the perceived threat to the survival of the Soviet Union. Throughout the period of the FYPs, the Soviet government asserted that the USSR was a nation under siege. It argued that unless priority was given to defence needs, the continued existence of the USSR could not be guaranteed. Set against such a threat, workers' material interests were of little significance. To demand improved living and working conditions at a time when the Soviet Union was preparing to fight for its very existence was portrayed as being tantamount to national betrayal. Therefore, although food shortages continued, severe overcrowding persisted and basic consumer goods remained unavailable, expenditure on armaments increased. Defence spending rose from 4% of the overall industrial budget in 1933 to 17% by 1937. By 1940, under the terms of the Third FYP which repeated its forerunners' commitment to heavy industrial development, this proportion had reached 33%. Despite the official adulation given to Stalin for his great diplomatic triumph in achieving the non-aggression Pact with Nazi Germany in August 1939, there was no relaxation within the Soviet Union of the war atmosphere; indeed, the conditions of the ordinary people became even harsher. An official decree of 1940 abolished what remained of the free labour market. Government direction of labour, restrictions on population movement, enforced settlement of undeveloped areas and severe penalties for slacking and absenteeism were some of the measures imposed under this regulation. In 1941, at the point at which the German invasion effectively destroyed the Third FYP, the conditions of the Soviet industrial workers were marginally lower than in 1928. But in 1941, and this in Soviet thinking was a far more significant consideration than the question of living conditions, the USSR was in a position economically to engage in an ultimately successful military struggle of unprecedented duration and intensity. This fact has become the standard argument advanced as an explanation and justification of Stalin's enforced industrialisation of the USSR.

In judging the scale of Stalin's achievement it is helpful to cite such statistics relating to industrial output during the period of the first three FYPs as are reliable. The following data are drawn from the work of the economic historian, E. Zaleski, whose findings are based on careful analysis of Soviet and Western sources:

	1927	1930	1932	1935	1937	1940
Coal (million tons)	35	60	64	100	128	150
Steel (million tons)	3	5	6	13	18	18
Oil (million tons)	12	17	21	24	26	26
Electricity (million Kwths)	18	22	20	45	80	90

4 The Economy During Wartime, 1941–45

The ferocious four-year war that began with the German invasion of

June 1941, destroyed all semblance of measured, centralised, planning. Henceforward every consideration, political or economic, was sacrificed to the sheer necessity of survival. After an initial paralysis of will, Stalin again began to exercise his formidable powers of leadership. In his first radio broadcast of the war (3 July 1941) he exhorted the people to defend 'Mother Russia' by adopting the scorched-earth methods of warfare that had never failed to save the nation in its glorious past:

1 The issue is one of life and death for the Soviet State, of life and death for the peoples of the USSR. We must mobilise ourselves and reorganise all our work on a new wartime footing, where there can be no mercy to the enemy.
5 We must strengthen the Red Army's rear, subordinating all our work to this end. All our industries must be made to work with greater intensity, to produce more rifles, machine-guns, cartridges, shells, planes; we must organise the guarding of factories, power stations, telephonic and telegraphic communica-
10 tions, and arrange local air-raid protection.
In case of a forced retreat of Red Army units, all rolling stock must be evacuated; the enemy must not be left a single engine, a single railway car, not a single pound of grain or gallon of fuel. The collective farmers must drive off all their cattle and turn over
15 their grain to the safe keeping of the state authorities for transportation to the rear. All valuable property, including non-ferrous metals, grain and fuel, that cannot be withdrawn must be destroyed without fail.
In areas occupied by the enemy, sabotage groups must be
20 organised to combat enemy units, to foment guerrilla warfare everywhere, to blow up bridges and roads, damage telephone and telegraph lines, to set fire to forests, stores and transports. In occupied regions, conditions must be made unbearable for the enemy.

*From 1941, Stalin's insistence during the previous 13 years that the Soviet economy put itself on a war footing began to show obvious benefits. Whatever the reality of central planning had been, the principle of authority exercised from the centre was of considerable value when it came to organising the war effort. Moreover, the strictness of the regime, and the harshness of the conditions under which the Soviet people had laboured in the 1930s, had the effect of preparing them for the fearful hardships brought by the war. There is much evidence to suggest that in the four bitter years of 'The Great Patriotic War' the raw courage and resilience of the Russian people, seemingly inured to suffering, proved a priceless asset.
The degree of suffering can be expressed very simply. After five months of fighting, nearly half the Soviet population and over a third of the nation's industrial plant was under German occupation; 60% of iron

and steel production, 40% of the railway system, 60% of livestock, and 40% of grain stocks had been lost. The reason for this early catastrophe was that under the FYPs Soviet industrial expansion had been sited west of the Urals, the area most vulnerable to German attack. Extraordinary, and largely successful, efforts were subsequently made to transfer whole sectors of Soviet industry to the relative safety of the eastern USSR. Military conscription of all adult males not involved in essential war work, and war casualties (four million in the first year of the war), meant that women and children had to fill the vacant places in the factories. Work on the land became an almost totally female activity. Arms production received top priority. By 1942 55% of national income was being devoted to military expenditure. This was the highest proportion by far of any of the countries involved in the Second World War. In such straitened circumstances the pre-war levels of production could not be maintained. The following figures suggest the scale of industrial disruption caused by the German occupation during the first two years of the war:

	1940	1942
Coal (million tons)	150	75
Iron (million tons)	15	4
Steel (million tons)	18	8
Oil (million tons)	26	22
Electricity (million Kwths)	90	29

*1942 marked the lowest point in Soviet economic fortunes. However, when things began to improve on the military front towards the end of that year, there was a corresponding improvement in the economic situation. The new factories in the Urals region began to come into production. The lend-lease programme of the USSR's ally, the USA, became effective, substantially complementing the Soviet's home-produced supply of weapons and motor transport. Of special significance was the recovery and expansion of the Soviet railway system, enabling the strategic and tactical movement of troops and supplies. With the retreat of the German armies on a broad front, following the major Soviet victories in 1943 at Stalingrad and Kursk, the USSR began to recover its lost industrial sites. The beneficial effects of all this on the Russian war economy had become obvious by the last year of the conflict.

Wartime Productivity in the USSR
(calculated to a relative base unit of 100 in 1940)

	1941	1942	1943	1944
National Income	92	66	74	88
Total Industrial Output	98	77	90	104
Armaments Production	140	186	224	251
Fuel Production	94	53	59	75
Agricultural Output	42	38	37	54

*These figures indicate the prodigious response of the Soviet Union to the demands of war. The ability to achieve a huge arms production at a time of acute shortages in plant, materials and manpower is the outstanding example of this response. However, behind the data lies the reality of a measure of privation for the Soviet people greater than they had already undergone during collectivisation and industrialisation. The long German occupation of the most fertile lands, the shortage of agricultural labour, the re-imposition of State grain and livestock requisitions and the disruption of the food distribution system: these combined to transform the chronic Russian food shortage into famine. Of the twenty million Soviet citizens who died as a result of the war, it is calculated that about five million starved to death. Even so, Stalin had the last word. As the military struggle drew to its successful close in May 1945, he declared: 'We have survived the most cruel and hardest of all wars ever experienced in the history of our Motherland. The point is that the Soviet social system has proved to be more capable of life and more stable than a non-Soviet system.'

6 Postwar Reconstruction

The appalling sufferings of the Soviet population had not diminished Stalin's grip upon the country. Indeed, the Soviet victory and his part in it had made his position within the USSR unassailable. When Stalin turned to the consideration of Soviet economic reconstruction after the ravages of war, it was with no thought of rewarding the people for their efforts. If anything, he was even more suspicious of the outside world than he had been before 1941. He called upon the nation to redouble its efforts. Defence and the recovery and expansion of heavy industry were again to be the priorities. Little appeared to have changed in his economic thinking since 1928. Adjustments were made in the structure and personnel of the central planning departments but these were of only minor importance; the basic economic strategy remained the same.

At the end of the war it appeared that the Soviet Union now had extra resources it could tap. The recovery of all its territory, its entitlement to large-scale reparations from defeated Germany and its hold over the Eastern European states it claimed to have liberated during the war, gave promise of enhanced economic stability. However, against that had to be set the degree of disruption caused by the war. The Fourth FYP (1946–50) was aimed at restoring production to the levels of 1941. Even allowing for inflated claims, this seems largely to have been achieved within three years. But, as had been the case with the earlier Plans, the goals were reached only in the traditional areas of heavy industry. The Soviet economy itself remained unbalanced. In those sectors where unskilled and forced labour could be easily and effectively used, as in war-damage clearance and the re-building of abandoned factories and plants, the results were impressive. However, there was little recognition of the need to adapt to progressive industrial techniques, despite the post-war presence in the USSR of United Nations economic advisers sympathetic to Soviet needs. Stalin continued to be committed to large-scale, visually-striking, construction projects. Bridges, dams, refineries, and generating plants took pride of place in the Plan, but without much thought being given to their integration into an overall economic strategy. Their construction often involved the wasting of vital financial and material resources that could have been invested elsewhere far more productively. These showpieces, collectively termed 'Stalin's Grand Projects of Communism', had more to do with Stalinist propaganda than genuine economic planning. The same consideration may be said to apply to the successful detonation in 1949 of the Soviet Union's first atomic weapon.

*When such reservations have been made about the imbalance of Soviet planning, the fact remains that by 1950 the Fourth FYP had realised its objectives in regard to the growth of heavy industry; the output of iron and steel, oil and electrical power had been doubled. The major weakness, as with the pre-war Plans, was the inability to increase agricultural productivity or to raise the living standards of the Soviet workers. Lip-service was paid to these two aims in both the Fourth and Fifth FYPs (the latter, 1951–55, outliving Stalin), but, in practice, little was done. Agriculture continued to be under-capitalised and regarded as wholly secondary to the industrial programme. It is true that in the early 1950s Khrushchev was given a special commission to investigate the problems of the collective farms but his task was largely to enforce political conformity in the countryside rather than improve food yields. Rationing had been formally ended in 1947 but this was not a real sign that shortages had been overcome; a widespread black-market, officially condemned but tolerated in practice, was necessary for the workers to supplement their meagre resources. Scarcity of accommodation continued as an apparently insoluble problem, and life in the factories was no less harsh than it had been in wartime. Real wages were not permitted to rise above subsistence level and the rigours of the 'Labour Code' were not relaxed. When Stalin died in 1953 the lot of the Russian worker, the concept of whose material improvement had been the inspiration of the October Revolution, was arguably harsher than at any time since 1917.

Making notes on 'Stalin and the Soviet Economy'

In compiling your notes, concentrate on gaining an understanding of essentials. The key point to bear in mind is that in the Soviet Union, even more than in most countries, political and economic questions overlapped. The following list of headings and questions will help to order your thoughts:

1 **Background:** What do you understand by the terms 'the Second Revolution' and 'Revolution from above'? Why were there serious disagreements among the Bolsheviks about the way the Soviet economy should develop? What special economic problems confronted post-Leninist Russia?

2 **Collectivisation:** Who were the 'Kulaks'? What were the motives behind Stalin's collectivisation programme? Describe the main features of that programme. What do the various tables on pages 32 and 33 tell you about the scale of collectivisation? Why was there a particularly severe famine in the USSR in the years 1932–33? Were there any genuine alternatives to Stalin's policy of collectivisation?

3 **Industrialisation:** In what sense did industrialisation introduce a 'war economy'? Why did Stalin lay such stress on the development of heavy industry?

   a) **1st FYP:** Distinguish between the 'optimal' and the actual Plan. What methods were used to achieve the Plan's targets? Was the 1st FYP 'an economic model'?

   b) **2nd and 3rd FYPs:** Did the 2nd and 3rd FYPs differ significantly from the 1st? How were Stakhanov's achievements used in the official Soviet propaganda of the time? Why, despite the Plans, did the living standards of Soviet workers decline in this period?

4 **The Debate on Stalin's Policies:** What are the major points of difference between historians in their judgement of a) Stalin's aims, and b) his methods? How would you accont for such differences of view?

5 **The Economy in Wartime:** What impact did the war have on Soviet economic planning? In what sense was 1942 a turning point in Soviet economic fortunes? Was the Soviet economy stronger in 1945 than it had been in 1941?

6 **Postwar Reconstruction:** What influence did the postwar international situation have on Stalin's economic attitudes? What was meant by the term 'Stalin's Grand Projects of Communism'? Do the 4th and 5th FYPs indicate any basic alteration in Soviet industrial strategy?

Answering essay questions on 'Stalin and the Soviet Economy'

The economic changes associated with Stalin's policies after 1928 mark a significant turning-point in the development of modern Russia. The introduction of collectivisation and industrialisation created 'the Second Revolution', a term which suggests that these processes were as important as the Revolution of 1917 itself. Consequently, the topic is regarded as main-stream and is highly popular with examiners. Ques-

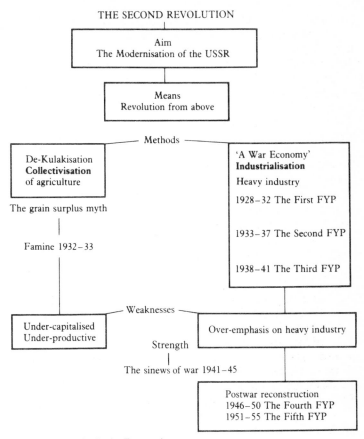

THE SECOND REVOLUTION

Aim
The Modernisation of the USSR

Means
Revolution from above

Methods

De-Kulakisation
Collectivisation
of agriculture

The grain surplus myth

Famine 1932–33

'A War Economy'
Industrialisation

Heavy industry

1928–32 The First FYP

1933–37 The Second FYP

1938–41 The Third FYP

Weaknesses

Under-capitalised
Under-productive

Over-emphasis on heavy industry

Strength

The sinews of war 1941–45

Postwar reconstruction
1946–50 The Fourth FYP
1951–55 The Fifth FYP

Summary – 'Stalin and the Soviet Economy'

tions are frequently set which call for a knowledge of the major developments and an understanding of their significance. In History A-Level papers, while you are not required to wrestle with the more sophisticated aspects of economic theory, you are expected to show an awareness of the great importance of economic factors in Stalin's Russia. After all, the major issues in Soviet politics were basically economic ones. How was a revolutionary country which had rejected capitalism to survive in a capitalist world? How could the Soviet Union best use its resources to ensure that survival? Could a country that was predominantly rural and agricultural be transformed into a modern industrial state? It is unlikely that you would be asked such questions in a direct form, but you need to understand that these were the problems that lay at the heart of Soviet politics. Stalin's personal role is, of course, vital and it makes sense for you to concentrate on the central theme: what were Stalin's economic aims and how far did he achieve them? In pursuing that line of questions you will necessarily have to study all the essential features of the Russian economy between 1928 and 1953.

If, in accordance with the earlier suggestions, you have already made effective notes on this chapter you will be in a position to get the best from the following approach:

Aims –   1 What were Stalin's main objectives in embarking upon a policy of collectivisation and industrialisation?

2 In what sense did the policies of collectivisation and industrialisation constitute 'a Second Revolution' in the Soviet Union?

Methods – 3 'By 1933 the material conditions of the Soviet people had reached an unprecedentedly low level.' How far were Stalin's economic policies responsible for this situation?

4 How accurate is it to describe the First Five-Year Plan (1928–32) as an 'economic model'?

Results – 5 'That the USSR was able to survive the war of 1941–45 was entirely due to Stalin's successful reconstruction of the Soviet economy by 1941.' Discuss.

6 Consider the view that 'compared with his earlier years of planning, Stalin's economic policies after 1945 are oddly shapeless'.

Here is a suggested essay plan for question 2: (1) Begin with a list of the principal economic and social changes brought about by the two policies; these should include such points as the anti-Kulak campaign, the expropriation of peasant holdings, the migration from the land to the towns, the creation of major industrial enterprises and the development of heavy industry. (2) From this list you can then fashion the main features of the collectivisation and industrialisation process. (3) With these as ammunition you should then be able to attack the more important (and more difficult) part of the question; namely, to put the idea of 'a Second Revolution' in the context of Bolshevik revolutionary theory. Define what the first Revolution was in Bolshevik eyes – the triumph of the urban proletariat. (4) With that established you can then go on to suggest that collectivisation and industrialisation were Stalin's way of ensuring that what had been achieved in 1917 would not be lost, that the peasants would be made to serve the interests of the proletariat in Revolutionary Russia's drive towards modernisation, and that the Soviet State would assume total control. For Stalin the 'Second Revolution' that he initiated was as necessary and as significant as the first Revolution in 1917 had been. (5) You are, of course, entitled (and, indeed, should be so encouraged) to take a critical view of Stalin's policies. Provided that an answer kept within the terms of the question, one that challenged the logic of Stalin's concept of a 'Second Revolution' would appeal to examiners as a mature and thoughtful response.

Source-based questions on 'Stalin and the Soviet Economy'

1 Stalin justifies the pace of change, 1931

Study the extract from Stalin's speech on page 29 and then answer the following questions:
a) What reasons does Stalin give for refusing to contemplate a slowing down of the tempo of economic development?
b) Identify the weaknesses, as Stalin sees them, of traditional Russia.
c) From your own knowledge, how sincere would you judge Stalin to be when he speaks of 'our obligation to the working class of the whole world'?
d) In what ways is this extract valuable to the historian who is studying the motivation behind Stalin's economic policies?

2 The First Five-Year Plan

Examine the table of figures on page 37, the illustration on page 39 and the description of Magnitogorsk on page 37 and then answer the following questions:
a) From your own knowledge, suggest reasons why there are four separate sets of figures for the FYP.
b) What other type of evidence would you need to examine in order to put the quoted figures in perspective?
c) A number of key features of Stalin's industrialisation drive are contained in the Magnitogorsk description. Identify these.
d) The poster illustrates the internal and external enemies of Stalin's industrialisation plans. Suggest what groups are being depicted.
e) How could these three sources be used to construct an analysis of the aims and effects of the FYPs?

3 The Soviet Economy at war

Study the extract from Stalin's broadcast on page 44 and the sets of statistics on page 45 and then answer the following questions:
a) In what ways does Stalin's broadcast illustrate what is meant by a 'scorched earth' policy?
b) What evidence is offered by the first table on page 45 of the immediate changes forced on the economy by the onset of war in 1941?
c) Using your own knowledge, and the statistics of wartime productivity on page 45, judge how successfully the Soviet economy adapted itself to the demands of war in the years 1941–44.
d) With what reservations would you approach the statistics relating to developments in Soviet agriculture and industry given in this chapter?

CHAPTER 4

Stalin and Political Power

Stalin had achieved power in the Soviet Union by 1929, with his defeat of the Left and Right Bolsheviks. He subsequently consolidated that power to the point of absolutism by a series of purges that continued right up to his death in 1953. In theory, a purge was a means of purifying and preserving the Communist Party and the Soviet State. It worked, in practice, by demoting or removing members and officials whose ideas or behaviour were considered by Stalin to be a challenge to his own authority. It was his mastery over the machinery of Party and government, rather than any post he held as nominal head of State, that enabled Stalin to use the purge as a devastatingly effective instrument of political control.

1 The Earlier Purges

The Stalinist purges which began in 1934 were not unprecedented. During the 1920s tens of thousands of anti-Communists, variously dubbed by the authorities as 'bourgeois nationalists', 'Left-wing anti-Bolsheviks' and 'deviationists', had been imprisoned in labour camps. It is also possible to interpret the defeat of the Left and Right in the power struggle of the 1920s as successful Stalinist purges. Stalin wanted to take stern measures against those he had overcome, but he was prevented from doing so by the intercession of the other members of the Politburo. That he allowed himself to be dissuaded suggests that he did not yet consider himself to be in full control.

Public trials, such as the Shakhty affair (see page 38), had been held during the early stages of the First Five Year Plan as a way of identifying and disgracing industrial 'saboteurs'. However, even at this early stage, prosecutions had not been restricted to industrial enemies. In 1932 the trial of the Ryutin group had taken place. These were the followers of M. N. Ryutin, a Right Bolshevik, who had published an attack on Stalin, describing him as 'the evil genius who had brought the Revolution to the verge of destruction'. Ryutin and his supporters were publicly tried and expelled from the Party. This was the prelude to the first major purge of the CPSU by Stalin. Between 1933 and 1934 nearly one million members, over a third of the total membership, were excluded from the Party on the grounds that they were 'Ryutinites'.

*At the beginning, Party purges were by no means as violent and deadly as they later became. They did not always take the form of legal proceedings; neither did they necessarily involve formal dismissal from the Party, let alone imprisonment or execution. The usual procedure was to require members to hand in their Party cards for checking, at which point any suspect individuals would not have their cards returned to them. In effect, this amounted to expulsion since, without cards, members were denied access to all Party activities; furthermore, they and their families then found it impossible to retain employment, housing or food-ration cards. The threat of expulsion was enough to force members to conform to official Party policy. Under such a system, it became progressively difficult to mount effective opposition. Despite this, attempts were made in the early 1930s to criticise Stalin, as the Ryutin affair illustrates. These efforts were ineffectual, but they prompted Stalin to believe that a serious, organised, challenge to his authority was still possible.

1934 is an important date in Stalin's rise to absolute authority. That year marks the point at which he began the systematic terrorising not of obvious political opponents but of colleagues and party members. It is difficult to explain precisely why Stalin initiated such a terror. Historians accept that they are dealing with behaviour that goes beyond reason and logic. Stalin was deeply suspicious by nature and right up to his death twenty years later he continued to believe himself to be under threat from actual or potential enemies. One historian, Alec Nove, offers this suggestion as to how Stalin's mind may have worked: 'The revolution from above caused great hardships, coercion left many wounds. Within and outside the Party, they might dream of revenge. Party leaders rendered politically impotent might seek to exploit the situation. So: liquidate them all in good time, destroy them and their reputations.' No one was safe; everyone was suspect. Purges became not so much a series of episodes as a permanent condition of Soviet political life. Terror became an all-pervading influence. The intensity of it varied from time to time, but it was an ever-present reality throughout the remainder of Stalin's life.

2 The Post-Kirov Purges, 1934–36

The pretext for the purge of 1934, which set the pattern for all subsequent persecutions, was the assassination of Sergei Kirov, the secretary of the Leningrad Soviet. The strong probability is that the death-plot against Kirov had been sanctioned by Stalin himself. Nikita Khrushchev in his secret speech in 1956, which began the process of de-Stalinisation (see page 99), stated that Stalin was almost certainly behind the murder. That is also the conclusion of the modern historian, Robert Conquest, who has made a special study of the incident. Stalin's motives are not hard to adduce. Kirov was a popular figure in the Party. A strikingly-handsome Russian, he had made a strong impression at the 17th Party Congress in 1934 and was subsequently elected to the Politburo. He was known to be unhappy with the current industrialisation drive, siding with those who were worried by the sheer pace of Stalin's programme. He was also opposed to extreme measures being used as a means of disciplining Party members. If organised opposition to Stalin were to form within the Party, Kirov was an outstanding example of the type of individual around whom dissatisfied Party members might rally. Whatever the degree of his involvement, Stalin certainly seized the opportunity that the assassination provided. Under the guise of exacting retribution for Kirov's murder, a fresh purge of the Party was begun. Stalin claimed that Kirov's death had been organised by a wide circle of Trotskyites and Leftists, who must all be brought to account. This justified a large-scale round-up of the suspected conspirators and their associates, followed by their imprisonment or execution. The atmosphere is captured in an account by Victor Serge, one of the 'oppositionists' who managed to flee from the USSR at this time:

1   I am convinced that at the end of 1934, just at the moment when Kirov was murdered, the Politburo was entering upon a policy of normality and relaxation. The shot fired by Nikolayev [the assassin] ushered in an era of panic and savagery. The immediate
5   response was the execution of 114 people, then the execution of Nikolayev and his friends; then the arrest and imprisonment of the whole of the former Zinoviev and Kamenev tendency, close on 3000 persons, as far as I could make out; then the mass deportation of tens of thousands of Leningrad citizens, simul-
10 taneously with hundreds of arrests among those already deported and the opening of fresh secret trials in the prisons. On Niko-layev's crime, the world has seen the publication of a number of successive versions, all of them lavish in improbabilities, but not of the original papers, whether the terrorists' own statements or
15 the documents of the investigation. It was almost certainly an individual act committed by an enraged Communist. The Left or Trotskyite Opposition had nothing whatever to do with the assassination.

*It is an interesting coincidence that just as Stalin's path to power had been smoothed ten years earlier by 'the Lenin enrolment' (see page 13), so in 1934 his successful purge had been made a great deal easier by a recent significant shift in the composition of the Party. During the previous three years the CPSU had recruited into its ranks a higher proportion of skilled workers and industrial managers than at any time since 1917. Stalin encouraged this as a means of tightening the links between the Party and those actually responsible for operating the First Five Year Plan (FYP), but it also had the result of introducing into the CPSU a considerable number of members who were career-orientated rather than politically-motivated. Conscious that their newly-acquired privileges and greater job prospects were a direct consequence of Stalin's patronage, such members were more than willing to support the elimination of the anti-Stalinist elements in the Party. After all, it improved their own chances of promotion. The competition for jobs in Soviet Russia was invariably fierce. Purges always left posts to be filled. Norman Stone expresses it in this form: 'It was characteristic of Stalin to have his own allies "marked" by their own subordinates: in Stalin's system identical thugs kept on replacing each other, like so many Russian dolls'. As the chief dispenser of positions, Stalin knew that the self-interest, if not the political conviction, of these new Party members would keep them loyal to him.

It was not difficult to find eager subordinates to organise the purges. The common characteristic of those who led Stalin's campaigns was their unswerving personal loyalty to him, a loyalty that overcame any scruples they might have had regarding the nature of their work. They were an unsavoury group of individuals whose marked lack of cultural refinement or moral sensibility added to the detestation and terror in which they were held by their victims. The preliminary purge in 1933 was arranged by Yezhov, chief of the Control Commission, the branch of the Central Committee responsible for Party discipline. The full-scale purge that followed Kirov's murder in 1934 was the work of Yagoda, head of the newly-formed NKVD, which had superseded the OGPU in that year as the State security force. In 1935 Kirov's key post as Party boss in Leningrad was filled by Zhdanov, described by one contemporary Communist, who managed to escape the purges, as 'a toady without an idea in his head'; the equivalent position in Moscow was filled by another ardent Stalinist, Nikita Khrushchev. In recognition of his strident courtroom bullying of 'oppositionists' in the earlier purge trials, Andrei Vyshinsky, a reformed Menshevik, was appointed State Prosecutor. Stalin's fellow-Georgian, Lavrenti Beria, was entrusted with overseeing State security in the national minority areas of the USSR. With another of Stalin's proteges, Poskrebyshev, in charge of the Secretariat there was no significant area of the Soviet bureaucracy which Stalin did not control. Public or Party opinion meant nothing when set against Stalin's grip on the key personnel and functions in Party and government. There had been rumours, around the time of the second FYP, of a possible move to oust him from the position of Secretary General. These were silenced in the aftermath of the Kirov affair.

★The outstanding feature of the post-Kirov purge was the eminent status of many of its victims. Prominent among those arrested were Kamenev and Zinoviev, who, along with Stalin, had formed the triumvirate after Lenin's death in 1924 and who had been the leading Left Bolsheviks in the power struggle of the 1920s. At the time of their arrest in 1935 they were not accused of involvement in Kirov's assassination, only of having engaged in 'opposition', a charge that had no precise meaning. However, the significance of their arrest and imprisonment was plain to all; no Party members, whatever their rank or revolutionary pedigree, were safe. What gave Yagoda and the operators of the purge such sweeping powers was the government's 'decree against terrorist acts', issued after Kirov's murder, which made the NKVD a law unto itself in its pursuit of the enemies of the State and the Party. Arbitrary arrest and summary execution became the norm. In the post-Stalin years it was admitted by Khrushchev that the decree had become the justification for 'broad acts which contravened socialist justice', a euphemism for mass murder. An impression of this can be gained from glancing at the fate of the representatives at the party Congress of 1934. Of the 1,996 delegates who attended, 1,108 were executed during the next three years. In addition, out of the 139 Central Committee members elected at that gathering all but 41 of them were put to death during the purges. Leonard Schapiro, in his study of the CPSU, has described these events as 'Stalin's victory over the Party'. From this point on, the Soviet Communist Party was entirely under his control. It ceased, in effect, to have a separate existence. Stalin had become the Party.

3 The Great Purge, 1936–39

In logic, it might be expected that once Stalin's absolute supremacy over the Party had been established the purges would be stopped. In fact, the reverse happened; they increased in intensity. Stalin declared that the Soviet Union was in 'a state of siege' and urged still greater vigilance in unmasking the enemies within. In 1936 there began a progressive terrorising of the Soviet Union which affected the entire population but which took its most dramatic form in the public show trials of Stalin's former Bolshevik colleagues. The one-time heroes of the 1917 Revolution and the Civil War were arrested, tried, and executed as enemies of the State. Remarkably, the great majority went to their death after confessing their guilt and accepting the truth of the charges levelled against them. Such was the scale of the persecution at this time, and so high ranking were the victims, that it has gone down in history as 'the Great Purge'.

The descriptions applied to the accused during the purges bore little relation to political reality. 'Right', 'Left' and 'Centre' opposition blocs were identified and the groupings invariably had the catch-all term 'Trotskyite' tagged on to them, but such words were convenient prosecution labels rather than definitions of a genuine political opposition. They were the preliminary means of identifying and isolating those in the Communist Party and the Soviet State whom Stalin wished to destroy.

a) The Purge of the Party

There is a similarity between the purges of the 1930s and the post-Lenin power struggle of a decade earlier. In each case it was the

Left who first came under attack, followed by an assault on the Right. The prelude to the Great Purge of 1936 was a secret letter sent from CPSU headquarters, warning all the local Party branches of a terrorist conspiracy by 'the Trotskyite–Kamenevite–Zinovievite–Leftist Counter-Revolutionary Bloc' and instructing Party officials to begin rooting out suspected agents and sympathisers. Once this campaign of denunciation and expulsion had been set in motion in the country at large, Kamenev and Zinoviev were put on public trial in Moscow charged with involvement in Kirov's murder and with plotting to overthrow the Soviet State. Both men pleaded guilty and read their abject written confessions in court. The obvious question is 'Why did they confess?' After all, these men were tough Bolsheviks. No doubt, as was later revealed during de-Stalinisation, physical and psychological torture was used. Possibly more important was their sense of demoralisation at having been accused and disgraced by the Party to which they had dedicated their lives. In a curious sense, their admission of guilt was a last act of loyalty to the Party.

Whatever their reasons, and these continue to be a puzzle to historians, the fact that they did confess made it extremely difficult for other victims of the purges to plead, or even to believe in, their own innocence. If the great ones of State and Party were prepared to accept their fate, on what grounds could lesser men resist? The psychological impact of the public confessions of such figures as Kamenev and Zinoviev was profound. It helped to create an atmosphere in which innocent victims cravenly submitted in open court to false charges, and went to their death begging the Party's forgiveness. It also shows Stalin's astuteness in insisting on a policy of public trials. There is little doubt that Stalin had the power to conduct the purges without using legal proceedings, but, by making the victims deliver humiliating confessions while on public trial, he was able to reveal the scale of the conspiracy against him and to prove the need for the purging to continue. There was also a political bonus in that the victims' confessions invariably incriminated others, thereby easing the task of further detection and justifying the continuation of harsh measures.

*This soon became evident after Kamenev and Zinoviev, along with fourteen other Bolsheviks, had been duly executed in keeping with Vyshinsky's notorious demand as Prosecutor that they be shot 'like the mad dogs they are'. The details that the condemned had revealed in their confessions were used in the preparation of the next major strike, the attack upon the Right deviationists. Bukharin, Rykov and Tomsky were put under investigation, but not yet formally charged. The delay was caused by the reluctance of some of the older Bolsheviks in the Politburo to denounce their comrades. Stalin intervened personally to speed up the process. Yagoda, who was considered to have shown too much sensitivity in his recent handling of the 'Trotskyite–Zinovievite bloc', was replaced as head of the NKVD by the less scrupulous

Yezhov whose name, like Vyshinsky's, was to become a by-word for terror.

*Meanwhile, the case for proceeding against Bukharin and the Right was strenghtened by the revelations at a further show trial in 1937, at which seventeen Communists, denounced collectively as the 'Anti-Soviet Trotskyist Centre', were charged with spying for Nazi Germany. The accused included Radek and Pyatakov, the former favourites of Lenin, and Sokolnikov, Stalin's Commissar for Finance during the First FYP. Radek's grovelling confession, in which he incriminated his close colleagues, including his friend, Bukharin, saved him from the death sentence imposed on all but three of the other defendants. (He died two years later in an Arctic labour camp.) Yezhov and Vyshinsky now had the evidence they needed. In 1938, in the third of the major show trials, Bukharin and Rykov (Tomsky had taken his own life in the meantime) and eighteen other 'Trotskyite-Rightists' were publicly arraigned on a variety of counts, including sabotage, spying and conspiracy to murder Stalin. The fact that Yagoda was one of the accused was a sign of the speed with which the terror was starting to consume its own kind. Fitzroy MacLean, a British diplomat, was one of the foreign contingent permitted to observe the trial. His description conveys the character and significance of the proceedings:

1 It was an impressive list [of defendants]: Bukharin, a former Secretary-General of the Communist International, for years the leading theorist of the Party and a close associate of Lenin; Rykov, Lenin's successor and Molotov's predecessor as Premier;
5 Yagoda who, until eighteen months ago, had been People's Commissar for Internal Affairs and supreme head of the all-powerful NKVD.

The prisoners were charged, collectively and individually, with every conceivable crime: high treason, murder, espionage and all
10 kinds of sabotage. They had plotted to wreck industry and agriculture, to assassinate Stalin, to dismember the Soviet Union for the benefit of their capitalist allies. They were shown for the most part to have been criminals and traitors to the Soviet cause ever since the Revolution – before it even. The evidence accumu-
15 lated filled no less than fifty large volumes. One after another, using the same words, they admitted their guilt: Bukharin, Rykov, Yagoda. Each prisoner incriminated his fellows and was in turn incriminated by them. There was no attempt to evade responsibility. They were men in full possession of their faculties;
20 the statements they made were closely reasoned and delivered with every appearance of spontaneity. And yet what they said, the actual contents of their statements seemed, to bear no relation to reality.

As the trial progressed, it became ever clearer that the under-

25 lying purpose of every testimony was to blacken the leaders of the
'bloc', to represent them, not as political offenders, but as
common criminals, murderers, poisoners and spies.

*At one point in the trial Bukharin embarrassed the court by
attempting to defend himself, but he was eventually silenced by
Vyshinsky's overbearing manner and was sentenced to be shot along
with the rest of the defendants. There is a particular irony attaching to
Bukharin's execution. Only two years previously he had been the
principal draftsman of the new constitution of the USSR. This 1936
Constitution, which Stalin described as 'the most democratic in the
world', was intended as a shop window to display to foreign Communists and Soviet sympathisers the legal propriety of the USSR. This was
the period in Soviet foreign policy (see page 78) when, in an effort to
offset the Nazi menace to the USSR, Stalin was urging the formation of
'popular fronts' between the Communist parties and the various
Left-wing groups in Europe. In addition to defining the relationship
between the independent federal Republics of the USSR, the 1936
Constitution claimed that socialism had been established and that there
were no longer any 'classes' in Soviet society; all exploitation having
ended, there were now only 'strata' of workers and peasants, working in
harmony for the mutual good of all. The basic civil rights of freedom of
expression, assembly, and worship were guaranteed. However, the true
character of Stalin's Constitution lay not in what it said but in what it
omitted to say. Hardly anywhere was the role of the Party mentioned;
its powers were not defined and, therefore, were not curtailed. It would
remain the instrument through which Stalin would exercise his total
control of the USSR. It is possible to argue that nowhere was the
fraudulent nature of Stalinism as a system of government more clearly
evident than in the Constitution of 1936. It was issued when the purges
were at their height. The contrast between its democratic claims and
the reality of the situation in the Soviet Union could not have been
greater.

b) The Purge of the Army

The targets of the purges were not restricted to Party members and
government officials. A significant development occurred in 1937 when
the Soviet military came under threat. Stalin's political control of the
Soviet Union would have been insufficient of itself to maintain his
authority if the armed services had continued as an independent force.
It was essential that they be kept subservient. Knowing that military
loyalties might make a purge of the army more dangerous and difficult
to achieve, Stalin took the preliminary step of organising a large
number of transfers within the higher ranks in order to lessen the
possibility of centres of resistance being formed when the attack came.

When this had been accomplished, in May 1937 Vyshinksy announced that 'a gigantic conspiracy' had been uncovered in the Red Army. Marshal Tukhachevsky, the popular and talented Chief of General Staff, was arrested along with seven other generals, all of whom had been 'heroes of the Civil War'. On the grounds that speed was essential to prevent a military coup, the trial was held immediately and in secret. The charge was treason; Tukhachevsky was accused of having spied for Germany and Japan. Documentary evidence, some of it supplied by German intelligence at the request of the NKVD, was produced in proof. The outcome was predetermined and inevitable. After ritual confession and condemnation, in June 1937 Tukhachevsky and his fellow generals were shot. There appears to have been a particularly personal element in all this. The President of the secret court which delivered the death sentences was Marshal Voroshilov, a devoted Stalinist, who had long been jealous of Tukhachevsky's superior abilities and greater popularity.

*The execution of Tukhachevsky was the signal for an even greater blood-letting. To prevent any possibility of a military reaction, a wholesale destruction of the Red Army establishment was undertaken. In the following 18 months all 11 War Commissars were removed from office; three of the five Marshals of the Soviet Union were dismissed; 75 of the 80-man Supreme Military Council were executed; 14 of the 16 army commanders, and nearly two-thirds of the 280 divisional commanders were removed; half of the commissioned officer corps, 35 000 in total, were either imprisoned or shot. It was reported that in some army camps at the height of the purge officers were taken away in lorry loads for execution. The Soviet Navy was also purged; all the serving admirals of the fleet were shot and thousands of naval officers were imprisoned in labour camps. The Soviet Air Force was similarly decimated, only one of its senior commanders surviving the purge.

The devastation of the Soviet armed forces, wholly unrelated to any conceivable military purpose, was complete by 1939. It left all three services severely undermanned and staffed by inexperienced or incompetent replacements. Given the defence needs of the USSR, a theme constantly stressed by Stalin himself, the deliberate crippling of the Soviet military is the aspect of the purges that most defies logic. It is the strongest evidence in support of the contention that Stalin had lost touch with reality.

c) The Purge of the People

Stalin's achievement of total dominance over Party, government, and military did not mean the end of the purges. The apparatus of terror was retained and the search for enemies continued. The purge technique was employed as a method of achieving the goals of the FYPs. There is a direct parallel between the persecution of Party members for political 'oppositionism' and the charges of industrial sabotage made against managers and workers in the factories. The purge was also a way of forcing the regions and nationalities into total subordination to Stalin. The show trials that had taken place in Moscow and Leningrad, with their catalogue of accusations, confessions, and death sentences, were copied in all the republics of the USSR. The terror they created was no less intense for being localised. For example, between 1937 and 1939 in Stalin's home state of Georgia, two state prime ministers were removed, four-fifths of the regional Party secretaries and thousands of lesser officials lost their posts, and there was a wide-ranging purge of the legal and academic professions. Foreign Communists living in the Soviet Union were not immune. Polish and German revolutionary exiles were rounded up in scores, and many of them were imprisoned or shot. The outstanding foreign victim was Bela Kun, the leader of the short-lived Communist revolution in Hungary in 1919. He was condemned and shot in 1936.

All areas of Soviet life were affected by the purges. The constant state of fear that they engendered conditioned the perception and responses of the whole Soviet people. It is fair to say that under Stalin terror was elevated into a method of government. Understandably, historians tend to concentrate on the central and dramatic features of the purges, such as the show trials and the attack upon the Party and the Red Army, but the greatest impact of the purges in terms of aggregate numbers was on the middle and lower ranks of Soviet society. One in eighteen of the population were arrested during Stalin's purges. Almost every family in the USSR suffered the loss of at least one of its members as a victim of the terror.

*In the headlong rush to uncover more and more conspiracies, to search out more and more culprits, interrogators themselves became victims and joined those they had condemned in execution cells and labour camps. Concepts such as innocence or guilt, truth and falsehood seemed to lose all meaning during the purges. The mass of the population were perplexed and disorientated. Fear, on the scale of that created by the purges, proved a great destroyer of moral values and traditional loyalties. The one aim was survival – even at the cost of betrayal. In an edition of the *Literary Gazette*, published in Moscow in 1988, and devoted to an examination of the Stalin purges, a Soviet writer bewailed 'the special sadism, the sophisticated barbarism, whereby the nearest relatives were forced to incriminate each other – brother to slander brother, husband to blacken wife'.

4 The Later Purges, 1941–53

The purges continued even in wartime, albeit in a less obvious manner. Stalin blamed military failures on internal sabotage and persecuted those deemed responsible. Neither the war nor its outcome lessened his vindictiveness. He emerged from the war harder in attitude towards the Soviet people, despite their heroic efforts on his behalf, and more suspicious of the outside world, despite the alliances entered into by the USSR. The undeniable fact that many Soviet troops had deserted to the enemy, particularly in the early phases of the war, provided the justification for a large-scale purge of the Soviet armed forces at the end of the war. At the Yalta and Potsdam Conferences in 1945 the Allies had agreed in principle that all released prisoners-of-war should be returned to their country of origin. In central and eastern Europe these included many Soviet citizens who had fought for Germany against the USSR in an attempt to break free of Stalin. Not unnaturally, they were terrified at the prospect of what awaited them and pleaded with their Allied captors not to be sent back. However, in the face of Stalin's insistence, the Allies gave in and forcibly repatriated the prisoners they held. The consequences were as appalling as the prisoners had anticipated. Mass executions took place on Stalin's orders. What deepened the tragedy was that the victims were not only fighting-men. On the grounds that whole communities had supported Hitler's forces, whole communities were made to suffer. It was at this time that the Cossacks as a people were virtually destroyed, as a punishment for their support of the German armies during the war. Stalin's retribution against those who had fought against him reached the proportions of genocide.

Stalin was scarcely gentler to the legitimate Soviet prisoners who returned from German captivity. He did not disguise his contempt for them, apparently believing that their very survival somehow indicated that they had collaborated with their captors. It was not uncommon in 1945 for prisoners to be released from German prison camps, only to be transferred directly into Soviet labour camps. Their callous treatment at his hands was further evidence that the purges would continue. The USSR's victory in the Great Patriotic War had not deflected Stalin from his policy of exacting absolute obedience from the Soviet people. The camps would remain. There would be the same unrelenting search for victims to fill them.

*His suspicion of the hostile designs of the West on the USSR, which had been deepened rather than diminished by his wartime contacts with Western leaders, led him to demand that still greater attention be given to Soviet state security. The Westward advance of the Red Army during the final stages of the war had left the USSR in occupation of large areas of central Europe. In one obvious sense this greatly added to Soviet strength. But Stalin's determination at the end of the war to cling on to these regions and turn them into satellites created its own difficulties. It increased Cold War tensions between East and West and it widened the area of Soviet security fears. To balance this, Stalin insisted that the governments of the new Soviet bloc give priority to the establishment of a state security system capable of suppressing all forms of opposition to themselves and to the Soviet Union. The methods by which Stalin's Russia had been ruled during the previous 15 years became (with the single exception of Yugoslavia) the norm in the satellites. The national Communist Party, totally loyal to Stalin and the USSR and kept so by frequent purges, governed in each of the countries of the Soviet bloc. The sycophantic daily adulation of Stalin in the Soviet press was repeated in all the satellites. Stalin's was the living and unchallengeable voice of international Marxism–Leninism.

Such acclaim in no way lessened the rigidity of Stalin's outlook. Indeed, as he grew older he became more critical and suspicious of those around him, whether in party or government. After 1947 he dispensed with the Central Committee and the Politburo, thus removing even the semblance of limitation upon his authority. In 1949 he initiated another Party purge, 'the Leningrad Affair', comparable in scale and style to those of the 1930s. Leading Party and city officials, including those who had previously been awarded the title 'Hero of the Soviet Union' in honour of their courageous defence of Leningrad during the war, were arrested, tried on charges of attempting to use Leningrad as an opposition base and shot.

The Jews of the USSR were the next section of the population to be purged. He ordered what amounted to a persecution of the Jews for no better reason, apparently, than that his daughter, Alliluyeva, had had an affair with a Jew of whom he disapproved. Anti-Semitism was a long-established tradition in Russia and it was a factor in the last purge Stalin attempted. Early in 1953 it was officially announced from the Kremlin that a 'Doctors' Plot' had been uncovered in Moscow; it was asserted that the Jewish-dominated medical centre had planned to murder Stalin and the other Soviet leaders. Preparations began for a major assault on the Soviet medical profession, comparable to the pre-war devastation of the Red Army. What prevented those preparations being put fully into operation was the death of Stalin in March 1953.

5 The Dimensions of the Purges

Until the late 1980s it was not possible for historians, either inside or outside the USSR, to make accurate estimates of the number of victims of Stalin's purges. They were believed to run into millions, but nobody could be precise. However, in 1988 the KGB allowed certain of its archives recording the work of its forerunner, the NKVD, to be opened. An examination by Soviet historians of the relevant files produced the following calculations in regard to the Stalinist period:

> In **1934**, one million were arrested and executed in the first major purge, mainly in Moscow and Leningrad.
> By **1937**, 17 to 18 million had been transported to labour camps; 10 million of these died.

By **1939**, another five to seven million had been 'repressed', one million of these being shot, another one to two million dying in the camps.

In **1940**, the occupation of the Baltic states (Lithuania, Estonia and Latvia), Bukovina and Bessarabia resulted in two million being deported, most of whom died.

In **1941**, the deportation of various national groups, including Germans, Chechens and Crimean Tatars, led to the deaths of one third of the three million involved.

Between **1944** and **1946**, the 'screening' of returned prisoners of war and those who had been under German occupation resulted in 10 million being transported to labour camps; five to six million of these died in captivity.

Between **1947** and **1953**, one million died in the various purges and repressions during the last six years of Stalin's life.

6 The Purges in Perspective

Only a partial answer can be offered as to why Stalin undertook the purges. Reference can be made to his wish to consolidate his absolute authority by bringing all the organs of Party and State under his control but, even after he had achieved that aim, the terror continued. The purges were so wildly excessive and brutal that they defy logical analysis. However genuine the grounds he had for suspecting opposition, his fears revealed a deep irrationality amounting to paranoia. His daughter, Alliluyeva, hinted at this:

1 As he'd got older my father had begun feeling lonely. He was so
  isolated from everyone that he seemed to be living in a vacuum.
  He hadn't a soul he could talk to. It was the system of which he
  himself was the prisoner and in which he was stifling from
5 emptiness and lack of human companionship.

Psychology is a difficult area of historical research; it is not easy to judge an individual's mental processes. Nonetheless, there is enough external evidence to suggest that Stalin's behaviour was so unbalanced as to cast doubt on his sanity. That argument has been advanced in a number of major studies by the Kremlinologist, Robert Conquest. He finds Stalin's conduct to have been so arbitrary and out of keeping with the USSR's real needs as to be inexplicable in rational terms. Nor is this just the view of a Western liberal. In the freer atmosphere of the 1980s, Soviet writers began to acknowledge the enormity of Stalin's campaigns of terror. Building on the references made in Khrushchev's criticism of 'the cult of personality', they admitted that Stalin had been gratuitously cruel.

*When due allowance has been made for the mental and physical pressures applied to the accused, it has still to be explained why the great majority succumbed with so little resistance. Torture and coercion were not the whole story. We have to remember the role that the Party played in the lives of the Bolshevik old-guard. Most of the new recruits may have been time-servers and careerists, but for the old Bolsheviks of 1917 and the Civil War years membership of the CPSU was not merely a matter of political affiliation – it was a way of life. In medieval Christendom there was a saying 'Outside the Church there is no salvation'. That dogma may be suitably adapted to describe the attitude of the traditional Bolsheviks: 'Outside the Party there is no purpose to life'. It was their very dedication to the Party that led them to accept their fate. As individuals they knew they were innocent of the charges, but what did individuality matter when set against the collective truth of the Party? The Party's infallibility persuaded the condemned to accept the justice of the verdicts imposed on them. One of the old Bolsheviks, Yorykin, despite having been falsely charged, vilified, tortured and wrongly condemned, despite having seen his wife abused and his family deported, all on the personal orders of Stalin, could still cry out in the final seconds before he was shot 'Long live the Party, long live Comrade Stalin!' The Bolshevik mentality often baffles the judgement of the neutral historian, but there is enough evidence in the writings of Stalin's victims to indicate the peculiar power that the concept of Bolshevik loyalty exercised over the minds of Party members. Of course, not all the accused thought in this way. Many were helpless victims of what became a mass hysteria, which paralysed all thought of resistance and led individuals to try to escape by incriminating others. In such an atmosphere, in which guilt not innocence was assumed, an accusation was tantamount to proof. The witch-hunt principle was at work, and Stalin was the Witch-finder General.

Without seeking to deny that Stalin was the architect of the terror, a number of historians have begun to question whether Stalin was solely responsible for the purges. Their doubts have been prompted by the discovery that Stalinism, as a system of government, was not as monolithic as has been traditionally assumed. Attention has shifted to the disorganised state of much of Soviet bureaucracy, particularly at local level. While the decision to launch the purges was obviously taken by Stalin himself, how that decision was actually put into effect largely depended on the local Party organisation. It is arguable that the fragmentation and disruption of Soviet society, caused by the massive upheavals of collectivisation and industrialisation, destroyed any semblance of social stability and thereby encouraged Party and government officials to resort to the most extreme measures.

Making notes on 'Stalin and Political Power'

Your notes should help you to understand the way in which Stalin used the power which he held from the late 1920s onwards. Make a record of how the purges destroyed all possibility of opposition to him. Although the purges may be thought of as forming a single system of oppression, it is important that you note the differences between them. The following headings, sub-headings and questions should help you:

1   **The Earlier Purges**
1.1   How had the purges before 1934 been used to enforce Party loyalty?
2   **The Post-Kirov Purges**
2.1   The importance of Kirov's murder.
2.2   The type of Party member recruited to carry out the purges.
3   **The Great Purge**
3.1.1 The purge of the Left.
3.1.2 The purge of the Right.
3.2.1 Why did Stalin consider it necessary to purge the army?
3.2.2 The scale of the purge of the armed services.
3.3   The effects of the purge on the general population.
4   **The Later Purges**
4.1   Why did the purges continue after 1945?
4.2   The 'Leningrad Affair' and the 'Doctors Plot'.
5   **The Dimensions of the Purges**
5.1   How reliable are the statistics relating to the purges?
6   **The Purges in Perspective**
6.1   The problem of understanding Stalin's motives.
6.2   Why was there so little resistance to the purges?
6.3   Was Stalin solely responsible for the purges in the USSR?

Answering essay questions on 'Stalin and Political Power'

Although Stalin's exercise of power has been dealt with in this separate chapter, it is important to realise that it can be properly understood only in relation to the material in Chapters 2, 3 and 5. The purges are very closely connected to domestic, economic and foreign-policy matters and need to be seen in as broad a context as possible.

There are three fundamental issues in regard to Stalin's use of power, to which almost all other questions relate:
(a) What were Stalin's motives?
(b) By what means did he seek to achieve his aims?
(c) Why was there no effective resistance to him?

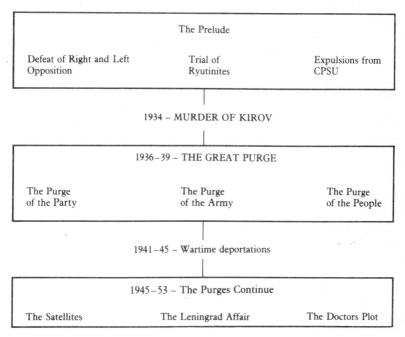

The Prelude

| Defeat of Right and Left Opposition | Trial of Ryutinites | Expulsions from CPSU |

1934 – MURDER OF KIROV

1936–39 – THE GREAT PURGE

| The Purge of the Party | The Purge of the Army | The Purge of the People |

1941–45 – Wartime deportations

1945–53 – The Purges Continue

| The Satellites | The Leningrad Affair | The Doctors Plot |

Summary 'Stalin and Power,

It is difficult for examiners to set a question on this topic which does not touch on at least one of these issues. In responding to the first question you would have to examine his aims as Soviet leader. This in turn leads to an analysis of the ways he put those aims into practice. In looking at those ways you become involved in studying why his methods were accepted and his orders obeyed. Put in very simple terms, you are asking: What did Stalin want to do? How did he go about it? How did he get away with it? If you shape your study around these three questions you are unlikely to ignore anything of real importance. Refer to the points you have already made in your notes and, if necessary, re-read the relevant parts of this and other chapters.

Consider the following A-Level questions:

1 Examine the methods by which Stalin made his power absolute in the Soviet Union.
2 What was the significance of the murder of Kirov in 1934?
3 'The real puzzle is not why Stalin conducted a policy of terror, but why the Soviet Union accepted it.' Discuss.
4 How acceptable is the view that 'the purges strengthened Stalin personally, but weakened the Soviet Union nationally'?

You will note that questions 1, 3 and 4 require you to discuss a wide range of factors, whereas question 2 concerns a specific event; of course to discuss 'significance' adequately you might well have to go beyond the limitations set by the title and date of the event.

Prepare an essay plan for question 2. Begin by drawing up a list of all the relevant points. These should include details of the political situation before the assassination, of the murder itself and of Stalin's reaction to it. Having drawn up your list, you should then begin to shape the points into an essay framework. Your opening paragraph should explain briefly how far Stalin had established his authority over the Party by 1934. The second paragraph should describe Kirov's standing in the Party and should suggest why Stalin saw this as a threat. A further short paragraph, describing what is known of the murder and Stalin's probable collusion in it, would be an appropriate lead-in to Stalin's public response to it. You are now in a position to explain, in two or three paragraphs, how Stalin used Kirov's assassination as a pretext to justify a wide-ranging and sustained purge of the Party, which became the pattern for all the subsequent purges. To give weight to your argument you should refer to the Great Purge of 1936–39. Your conclusion should emphasise the key points you have made, particular stress being laid on the murder being used as the justification for the extension of the purges of the CPSU.

Make two lists, one under the heading 'Stalin's methods' and one entitled 'the results'. You may care to sub-divide the first list into the various purges arranged in chronological or thematic order, e.g., Party, army, people. The second list could contain similar sub-divisions, relating to the groups or interests that Stalin brought under his control. It would be helpful if this list contained pointers as to why there was so little resistance to Stalin's methods.

Use the two lists you have compiled to plan answers to questions 1, 3 and 4. Question 1 requires an analysis of the methods Stalin employed to make his authority unchallengeable. Question 3 is essentially concerned with explaining why there were so few challenges, while question 4 asks you to consider whether the USSR as a nation gained or lost as a result of Stalin's terror. In each case aim to adapt the material contained in your lists to meet the demands of the particular question.

Source-based questions on 'Stalin and Political Power'

1 The Murder of Kirov 1934
Read the extract from Victor Serge's account on page 54 and then answer the following questions:
a) According to Serge, what immediate change in political attitudes was brought about by the assassination of Kirov?

b) What is Serge referring to when he uses the term 'The Left or Trotskyite Opposition' (line 17)?
c) How reliable would you judge Serge's comments to be? Of what value would this document be in a discussion of Stalin's responsibility for Kirov's murder?
d) Examine Stalin's likely reasons for attending as a mourner at Kirov's funeral.

2 A Show Trial 1938

Read the extract from Fitzroy MacLean's description on page 58 and then answer the following questions:
a) According to MacLean, what was remarkable about the list of defendants on trial?
b) What is the significance of MacLean's statement, in line 22, that 'their statements seemed to bear no relation to reality'?
c) What common features of the purges are illustrated in the particular show trial, as described by MacLean?
d) Using the evidence in the extract and your own knowledge, suggest reasons as to why the defendants all 'admitted their guilt' (line 16).

CHAPTER 5

Stalin and International Relations

1 Introduction

There is an important distinction to be made between the theory and the practice of Soviet foreign policy. Judged by its own propaganda, the Soviet Union was committed to the active encouragement of worldwide revolution. The Communist International organisation (Comintern) had been set up in 1919 in Moscow for this very purpose, to guide and co-ordinate the revolutionary movements in other countries. However, in practice the Bolsheviks did not regard Soviet Russia as being strong enough to sustain a genuinely revolutionary foreign policy. The first task was to ensure the survival of the Revolution in Russia itself. Between 1918 and 1921 the Bolsheviks were engaged in a desperate struggle to cling on to the power they had seized in 1917. The Civil War in Russia during those years gave Lenin and the Bolshevik Party little opportunity to organise revolution elsewhere. Whatever its claims may have been, the Comintern was concerned solely with safeguarding the interests of Soviet Russia.

After 1917, the Russian Communists found themselves in an odd situation. According to their own interpretation of Marxist theory, their revolution should have been quickly followed by proletarian seizures of power in many other countries. This did not happen. Indeed, at one time, the very reverse seemed about to take place. During the Civil War there occurred a series of armed interventions in Russia by France, Britain, the USA and Japan. These were overcome and were claimed by the Bolsheviks as a major triumph of Revolutionary Russia over her imperialist enemies, but they indicated that all thought of an immediate Soviet-backed proletarian revolution in other countries was unrealistic. Attempted Communist revolutions in Germany and Hungary were crushed by the authorities there. The Soviet Red Army entered neighbouring Poland in 1920 in the hope that the Polish workers would rise in revolution, but the Poles, viewing the Soviet troops not as proletarian liberators but as traditional Russian aggressors, threw them out. These reverses obliged Lenin and the Bolsheviks to reconsider their role as international revolutionaries.

Lenin's response was a practical one. He considered that for the present, since the capitalist nations were too strong and Revolutionary Russia was too weak, the Bolsheviks would have to modify Soviet foreign policy. For the time being Soviet Russia would have to co-exist with other countries. This did not mean that the Bolsheviks were abandoning all thought of international revolution, only that the time was not yet ripe for a full-scale attack on capitalism. Although Lenin was an outstanding revolutionary, he always retained a realistic approach to international politics. He was essentially a pragmatist, prepared to adjust his policies to the actual situation. He expressed this attitude in 1921, 'Our foreign policy while we are alone and while the capitalist world is strong consists in our exploiting contradictions.' The term 'exploiting contradictions' is an instructive one. What Lenin was saying was that Soviet Russia would protect itself in a hostile world by playing on the differences that separated the capitalist nations. The conflicting self-interest of such countries as France, Britain and Germany offered the opportunity to the Soviet Union of preventing the build-up of an anti-Bolshevik alliance among the capitalist powers. Fear of western encroachment was a long-standing feature of Russian foreign policy, going back to the days of the Tsars. That traditional anxiety was intensified by the bitter reaction of the governments of Europe to the 1917 Revolution and their calls for a crusade against Bolshevik Russia. In such a situation, with the USSR ever-conscious of its vulnerability, Soviet foreign policy was dominated by considerations not of aggression, but of defence. Compromise and survival, rather than provocation and expansion, were the foreign policies that Lenin handed down to Stalin.

*The starting point for the study of Soviet foreign policy under Stalin is the Treaty of Rapallo, signed between Germany and Soviet Russia in 1922. On the surface this was a surprising agreement between two countries opposed in character and outlook. The reason why Bolshevik Russia and reactionary Germany came together was simple necessity. They had no other choice. After 1918 they were both what Lloyd George, the British Prime Minister, called 'the pariah nations of Europe', the outcasts; Germany because of its defeat at the hands of the Allies in the Great War, and Russia because it had betrayed the Allies by making a separate and humiliating peace with Germany immediately following the Bolshevik take-over in 1917. It would be some time before either of these two nations would be accepted on equal terms by the victorious powers of the 1914–18 War. Germany and Russia were, therefore, thrown together. As outcasts, each had something to offer the other. The Rapallo agreement, by secretly providing German forces with training grounds in Russia, enabled Germany to flout the military restrictions imposed on her by the Versailles Treaty. Russia, denied commercial contact with the rest of Europe, was able to compensate by means of the trading rights with Germany written into the Treaty. The mutual commercial and diplomatic benefits that the Treaty of Rapallo gave to both countries formed the basis of a Russo-German co-operation that survived until the Nazis took power in Germany in 1933. Stalin accepted the wisdom of the pro-German policy he inherited and made no attempt to alter it. When it was finally abandoned it was not on his initiative but followed from the virulent anti-Bolshevism of Hitler and the Nazis.

2 Soviet Foreign Policy, 1924–29

a) Anglo-Soviet Relations

Britain had been the first nation to give Revolutionary Russia anything approaching international recognition when, in 1921, it had signed a preliminary trade agreement with her. In 1924 moves were made on both sides to expand this into an Anglo-Soviet treaty. The joint discussions were given impetus by the coming into office in that year of the first Labour Party Government in Britain. In the face of criticism from the other parties and from the City, this Labour Government pressed on with the preparation of a draft treaty. What prevented its being ratified as a formal agreement was the scandal in Britain following the publication in *The Times*, in October, of the 'Zinoviev Letter':

1 **SOVIET PLOT: RED PROPAGANDA IN BRITAIN: RE-VOLUTION URGED BY ZINOVIEV: FOREIGN OFFICE BOMBSHELL**
Very Secret
5 To the General Committee, British Communist Party: Executive Committee: Third Communist International: Presidium
                                      15 September 1924, Moscow
Dear Comrades
The time is approaching for the Parliament of England to
10 consider the Treaty concluded between the Governments of Great Britain and the USSR, for the purposes of ratification. The proletariat of Great Britain must show the greatest possible energy in the further struggle for ratification and against the endeavours of the British capitalists to annul it. It is indispensable
15 to stir up the masses of the British proletariat, to bring into movement the army of unemployed proletarians. . . .
Armed warfare must be preceded by a struggle against the inclinations to compromise which are embedded among the majority of British workmen, against the ideas of evolution and
20 peaceful extermination of capitalism. Only then will it be possible to count upon complete success of an armed insurrection. . . .
It would be desirable to have cells in all the units of the troops, particularly among those quartered in the large centres of the country, and also among the factories working on munitions and
25 at military store depots. . . .
In the event of danger of war, it is possible to paralyse all military preparations of the bourgeoisie and make a start in turning an imperialist into a class war. . . .
The military section of the British Communist Party, so far as
30 we are aware, further suffers from a lack of specialists, the future directors of the British Red Army. It is time you thought of forming such a group. Turn attention to the more talented

military specialists, who have, for one reason or another, left the Services and hold Socialist views. . . .
35   Desiring you all success, both in organisation and in your struggle.
     With Communist Greetings,
     Zinoviev, President of the Presidium of the IKKI (Comintern)

*That this letter was subsequently proved to be a White Russian forgery is less significant historically than that so many were ready to be convinced at the time that it was a genuine expression of Bolshevik intentions. The reaction to the letter indicated the fearsome image that, since 1919, the Comintern had created for itself abroad as the representative of Soviet Russia. It showed that, as long as the Comintern maintained its aggressive stance, diplomatic and commercial relations would always have to be conducted under the shadow of the political threat posed by the USSR.

The Conservative Government of Stanley Baldwin, which took over in Britain in 1924 following the defeat of the short-lived minority Labour Government, regarded the Soviet threat as real, and immediately withdrew recognition of The Soviet Union. In 1926, following the General Strike in Britain, it formally accused the USSR of having improperly supported the strikers. In the following year Baldwin authorised a full-scale police raid on the London premises of a Russian trade delegation suspected of being the centre of a Soviet espionage ring. He justified the raid in a House of Commons speech:

1 For many months the Police, in collaboration with the military authorities, have been investigating the activities of a group of secret agents engaged in endeavouring to obtain highly confidential documents relating to the Armed Forces of Great Britain.
5 From information received and evidence obtained in the course of these investigations it became increasingly difficult to resist the conclusion that the agents were working on behalf of the Russian Trade Delegation, working at Soviet House, who arranged for the conveyance to Moscow of photographs or copies of the documents
10 obtained.

Charges and counter-charges between the two countries followed, creating deep acrimony, and resulting in Britain suspending diplomatic relations. Some improvement in relations occurred in 1929 when Ramsay MacDonald's second Labour Government took office. Formal recognition of the USSR was restored and a new commercial agreement was discussed.

What Anglo-Soviet relations in the 1920s illustrate is that the activities of the Comintern ran counter to the diplomatic and commercial interests of the Soviet Union. It is one of the paradoxes of the period that, although the Comintern contrived to disturb other nations and so undermined Soviet trading prospects, it was never in a position seriously to advance the cause of international Communism. The result was that the Soviet Union got the worst of both worlds.

b) Stalin and International Communism

An obvious question arises as to why Stalin did not do more to prevent this. The answer is that he had little interest in other countries. He had scarcely been out of Russia and in no respect did he have the knowledge and experience of foreign affairs that marked both Lenin and Trotsky. Stalin had inherited the Comintern as the body responsible for co-ordinating schemes for international revolution but, except where it impinged on matters inside the Soviet Union, he paid scant attention to its activities. His momentous decision to adopt 'Socialism in One Country' required that foreign policy be subordinated to the interests of the Soviet Union. The Comintern continued to have a role under Stalin but it was limited to protecting the security of the USSR. It is significant that foreign Communist parties wishing to affiliate to the Comintern had formally to pledge themselves to absolute loyalty and obedience to the line dictated by the Soviet Union. Zinoviev coined the term 'Bolshevisation' to describe this process of subjecting international Communist parties to the will of Moscow. Far from being the vanguard of international Communism, the Comintern became a branch of the Soviet foreign office. Trotsky made this very charge during the power struggle. He accused Stalin of abandoning world revolution by taking the soft option in foreign affairs and siding with the enemies rather than the supporters of proletarian revolution.

*The dispute between Stalin and Trotsky on this issue was at its most bitter in regard to events in China. In 1927 Mao Tse-tung and the Chinese Communists were involved in a desperate struggle for survival against the Nationalists, led by Chiang Kai-shek. These two Chinese revolutionary parties had previously been in alliance, but Chiang had openly declared his intention of exterminating the Communists. Despite this, Stalin insisted that the alliance, which the Comintern had been instrumental in forming, must be maintained. He reasoned that Mao's Communists were too few and insignificant to be able to mount a genuine revolution; their only hope was to ally with the Nationalists and work for revolution on a broad front. The true proletarian revolution would have to wait. Trotsky denounced this policy as betrayal, pointing out that Stalin's interpretation of the Chinese situation was precisely equivalent to the heresy of the Russian Mensheviks in 1917 when they had argued that Russia's proletarian revolution must be preceded by a bourgeois rising based on an alliance of all the progressive parties. He condemned Stalin as the grave-digger of the

Chinese revolution. However, Stalin's victory in the Soviet power struggle effectively silenced all internal criticism of his policy on China, which remained unchanged. Chiang's murderous purging of the Communists continued. Mao decided that Stalin and the Comintern were not worth dying for; he rejected their instructions and fled to safety, taking with him a distrust of Soviet motives that he was to retain for the rest of his life. The self-regarding nature of Stalin's attitude towards the Chinese Communists has been described by Isaac Deutscher, the biographer of Stalin and Trotsky. He writes of Stalin's willingness 'to sacrifice the Chinese Revolution in what [he] believed to be the interest of the consolidation of the Soviet Union'.

*1927 was not a good year for the Soviet Union. In addition to its difficulties with China and Britain, rumours of an impending invasion of Russia by the capitalist powers gained credence. In neighbouring Poland, Pilsudski, the national hero who had led the successful resistance to the Red Army in 1920, had become head of government and had begun to take a strongly pro-Western, anti-Soviet line. If there were to be a Western attack on the USSR, the strategic danger that a hostile Poland posed for the Soviet Union would be considerable. War scares were a recurrent feature of life in the Soviet cities, such as Leningrad and Moscow, but things were particularly tense in 1927. There are grounds for thinking that Stalin and the authorities deliberately encouraged popular fears so that they could alternately cow or rally the nation. However, this is not to suggest that the war scares were wholly manufactured. The Soviet Union's often antagonistic behaviour towards the capitalist countries frequently produced counter blasts, as in the British case, and meant that international tension never wholly slackened. Today's observer can see that the mutual fears of the time were greatly exaggerated. There was never a capitalist plot for a concerted attack upon the Soviet Union and there was never a possibility of a Soviet-organised international revolution. However to the people of the time their apprehensions were real enough, and it was this fact that determined their attitude.

*The USSR's difficulties with Britain and Poland did have one beneficial effect; they tended to bring the Soviet Union and Germany closer together, since both countries had good reason for fearing the rise of a powerful Poland. However even here things did not go as well as they might. Stalin, suspicious and untrusting by nature, found it difficult to accept German good faith. In 1925 he had been disturbed by the German signing of the Treaty of Locarno, a European agreement, which had, in effect, accepted Germany as an equal for the first time since her defeat in 1918 and opened the way to her becoming a member of the League of Nations. Although he made no effort to detach the USSR from the Rapallo Treaty on which Soviet–German relations were based, he initiated a number of investigations and trials of German nationals who had come to work in the Soviet Union. Historians agree that the grim record of persecution by Stalin's secret police of both Soviet nationals and foreign residents was a major influence shaping the fear and resentment in which the USSR was held by other nations. It tended to make nonsense of Soviet claims that the USSR was truly a workers' State in which exploitation and suffering had been eliminated.

3 Soviet Foreign Policy, 1929–33

Not everybody in the Western world took a sceptical view of the Soviet Union. There were those, usually on the political Left, who wanted to believe the best of Soviet Russia and who considered that its poor image was a deliberate distortion, perpetrated by the capitalist-controlled Western press. For instance, many in the British trade union movement remained staunchly loyal to what they regarded as the Soviet experiment in workers' rule. Their influence was one of the factors prompting the second Labour Government (1929–31) to renew contact with the USSR. In 1929 Ramsay MacDonald's Government restored formal British recognition of the Soviet Union. This was the prelude to the re-negotiation of a commercial treaty between the two countries.

On the surface, these represented major diplomatic and commercial advances, but the gains were lessened by developments inside the Soviet Union around this time. What might be called a Left-turn is noticeable from around 1929. Stalin's victory over Bukharin was associated with his adoption of a much tougher approach to relations with other countries. This Stalinist hard line was taken not so much towards the governments of those countries as towards the non-Communist parties of the Left. It was laid down that all alliances between the Moscow-recognised Communist parties and other progressive groupings must cease. Movements, such as the Labour Party in Britain and the Social-Democrats in Germany, and individual socialist leaders, such as Ramsay MacDonald and Leon Blum of France, were denounced as 'social-fascists' whose only purpose was to delay the progress towards genuine revolution. Oddly enough, real fascism, which had been established in Italy since 1922 and was beginning to grow menacingly in its Nazi form in Germany, was largely ignored.

*It is not easy to give a completely satisfactory explanation of the blindness of Stalin and the Soviet Union over this, but part of the answer may relate to the peculiar circumstances of the time. It was in the late 1920s and early 1930s that Stalin embarked on his massive collectivisation and industrialisation programme. This happened to coincide with the onset of the Great Depression in North America and Europe. The apparent success of Soviet economic planning contrasted with the crisis in the West, which seemed to herald the collapse of capitalism, could be interpreted as evidence of the superiority of the Soviet system. If this were, indeed, the case then the Soviet Union had less to fear than it had hitherto thought. It need not, therefore, bother to cultivate links with the non-Marxist socialist parties in order to broaden the basis of its protection in a hostile world. It could continue its policy of direct contact with the capitalist governments, playing upon their weaknesses and endeavouring to exploit the contradictions between them.

In the long term, Stalin and the USSR were to pay dearly for their earlier misunderstanding of developments in Germany. Before 1933, the year of Hitler's coming to power, Stalin considered that the Nazis were not strong enough to achieve their ends. He appears to have been misled by their title, National Socialist, into thinking that they might, nonetheless, perform a useful function in preparing the ground for an eventual workers' revolution in Germany. Accordingly, it made sense for the KPD (German Communist Party) to co-operate with the Nazis. He failed to grasp that the strength and appeal of Nazism derived from its nationalism, which made it fundamentally opposed to international Communism. Such lack of basic insight prevented him from seeing the need to organise, while there was still time, an alliance of German movements of the Centre and Left against the Nazi menace. Events were to show that the KPD's obedient carrying out of the Kremlin's orders not to ally with the Social Democrats, but instead to attack them as 'social fascists', had destroyed the one real chance of creating a political barrier to Nazi takeover in Germany.

4 Soviet Foreign Policy, 1933–39

Even after Hitler came to power in 1933, Stalin was still slow to read the signs. He tried to maintain the eleven-year-old German alliance. It required such developments as violent Nazi attacks upon KPD members and premises, open discussion among German diplomats of their country's expansion into the USSR, and the signing early in 1934 of a German–Polish non-aggression treaty, with its obvious threat to Soviet security, to convince Stalin finally that the spirit of Rapallo was dead. The anti-Bolshevik propaganda that the Nazis began to produce in Germany was hardly less rabid than their anti-semitism. The USSR's greatest fear returned – that of isolation. For the next five years Soviet foreign policy directed itself to the task of finding allies to off-set the German danger. This has sometimes been referred to as a 'turnabout' in Soviet policy, but the reality was that the USSR had no alternative. It was no longer possible to pursue a pro-German policy. Germany was no longer a means of security, but was now the main threat. Tactics may have changed, but the central strategy, first introduced by Lenin, of avoiding Soviet Russia's international isolation, remained.

One of the earliest opportunities for the USSR to lessen its isolation came with its admission into the League of Nations in 1934. The League provided a platform for the Soviet Union, led by its newly-appointed Foreign Commissar, Litvinov, to call for the adoption of the principle of collective security in international affairs. One of the fruits of this was an agreement in 1935 between the USSR, France and Czechoslovakia, promising 'mutual assistance' if one of the partners suffered military attack. Also in 1935 preliminary Soviet diplomatic contact was made with the USA. However, of more immediate significance was the decision, taken in that same year by the Comintern at its seventh and last Congress, to reverse its former policy of non-alignment with the Left. The Comintern now appealed for a 'popular front' in Europe of all progressive parties to combat fascism. This was truly a turnabout in policy but it came too late. The damage had been done. European socialists, previously abused by the Soviet Union as 'social fascists', were understandably reluctant to respond favourably to what they regarded as mere Soviet expediency in the face of German aggression. Nonetheless, Stalin pressed on with his efforts to rally international support. The new Constitution which he introduced in 1936 [see page 59] was essentially a piece of propaganda aimed at convincing the outside world that the USSR was an egalitarian and democratic society.

*The gains which the new approach in Soviet foreign policy achieved proved largely superficial. Collective security was impressive as a principle, but was wholly unsuccessful in practice in the 1930s. The basic weakness was that Europe's two most powerful states, France and Britain, were not prepared to risk war in order to uphold the principle. Without their participation there was no possibility of collective security becoming a reality. As the 1930s wore on and Germany became stronger the resolve of France and Britain to act as upholders of European security appeared, in Soviet eyes, to lessen. This was certainly the inference to be drawn from Anglo-French reaction to fascist aggression in the mid-1930s. The response of France and Britain to the Italian invasion of Abyssinia in 1935 was the Hoare-Laval Pact, an agreement which accepted all Italy's principal demands. When Hitler, in direct contravention of the Versailles Treaty, ordered his forces to re-occupy the Rhineland in 1936, Britain and France offered feeble protests but made no military moves to prevent the German takeover.

1936 was a very black year for the USSR's hopes of sheltering under collective security. In addition to the display of German aggression and Anglo-French weakness, the year also saw the creation of an international alliance aimed directly against the Soviet Union. The fascist nations, Germany, Italy and Japan, came together in November 1936 to form the Anti-Comintern Pact. The danger that this represented of a two-front attack on the Soviet Union was immense and seemed to negate all the efforts made by the Soviet Union since 1933 to establish its security. It had the effect of re-doubling Stalin's efforts to obtain reliable allies and guarantees. However, in his attempts to achieve this, Stalin was labouring under a handicap, largely of his own making. The plain fact was that Soviet Russia could not be trusted. Enough was known of the Stalinist purges in the USSR to make neutrals in other countries wary of making alliances with a nation where such treachery or such tyranny was possible.

*If Stalin made it difficult for neutrals and moderates to sympathise with the defence needs of the Soviet Union, he also put barriers in the way of those on the political Left in other countries who should have been his natural supporters. His pursuit of defence agreements with the capitalist powers led Soviet foreign policy into ambiguities that confused and alienated many Soviet sympathisers. This was especially so with regard to Stalin's attitude towards the Spanish Civil War (1936–39). The struggle in Spain was a complex affair, but the rest of Europe tended to see it in simple terms as a struggle between the Republican Left and the fascist Right, a reflection of the basic political divide in Europe. Stalin and the Comintern, in keeping with the new Soviet policy of encouraging anti-fascist 'popular fronts', sent agents into Spain to organise an alliance of pro-Republican forces. Stalin's motives and policies were mixed. By focusing on Spain he was probably hoping to divert foreign attention away from the current horrors of the Soviet purges. That the sending of Soviet military equipment to the Republican side was not simple generosity was indicated by the requirement that the Republic transfer the greater part of its gold reserves to the USSR in payment. The 'popular front' policy meant in practice that the Soviet Union required all the Republican contingents to subordinate themselves to Soviet direction. The Spanish Left came to resent the ascendancy that the Soviet Union tried to assert over the Republican cause and to doubt whether Russia really wanted the victory of the Spanish Republic. They were correct; Stalin was anxious not to see a major victory for Marxism in Spain. The explanation of this paradox lies not in Spain, but in Europe at large. Stalin feared that, if Communism were installed in south-western Europe, this would so frighten France and Britain that they might well react by forming an anti-Soviet front with Germany and Italy, the very consequence which Soviet foreign policy was committed to avoiding.

*Events in Spain had not taken their full course when they were overtaken by dramatic developments in central Europe. In the autumn of 1938 France, Britain, Italy and Germany signed the Munich agreement, the climax to the Czechoslovak crisis. Hitler had demanded that the Sudetenland, an area which in 1919 had been incorporated, against the will of the majority of its inhabitants, into Czechoslovakia, be restored to Germany. He had threatened invasion if his requirements were not met. Although Hitler's demand was another breach of the Versailles settlement, neither Britain nor France was prepared to go to war over the issue. The Munich agreement conceded all his major demands. This success came on top of his achievement, earlier in 1938, of the *Anschluss*, the incorporation of Austria into the Third Reich.

This was in direct defiance of the Versailles settlement, which had forbidden the unification of Germany and Austria. Munich was thus a further example of Hitler's ability to get his way in Europe by exploiting French and British irresolution. In the Western world the Munich settlement has customarily been seen as an act of 'appeasement', part of the Anglo-French policy of avoiding war by making timely concession to the aggressor. That was not the interpretation put upon it by Stalin. He viewed the Munich conference, to which the USSR had pointedly not been invited despite its formal alliance with Czechoslovakia of 1935, as a Western conspiracy. For him, Munich was a gathering of the anti-Soviet nations of Europe, intent on giving Germany a free hand to attack a diplomatically-isolated Russia. To forestall this happening, Soviet efforts to reach agreement with France and Britain were intensified. In the year following Munich, Litvinov and his successor as Foreign Minister, Molotov, delivered a series of formal alliance proposals to the French and British governments. These went unanswered. France and Britain could not bring themselves to trust Stalin. Both countries also genuinely considered that an alliance with Poland rather than the USSR offered the better protection against further German expansion.

5 The Nazi–Soviet Pact, 1939–41

At this point Soviet foreign policy went into dramatic reverse. In August 1939 Molotov and his German counterpart, Ribbentrop, signed the Nazi–Soviet Pact, a formal pledge by both countries to maintain peaceful relations with each other:

1 The Government of the German Reich and the Government of the USSR, desirous of strengthening the cause of peace between Germany and the USSR, have reached the following agreement.

   Article I. Both High Contracting Parties obligate themselves to
5 desist from any act of violence, any aggressive action, and any attack on each other, either individually or jointly with other powers.

   Article II. Should one of the High Contracting Parties become the object of belligerent action by a third power, the other High
10 Contracting Party shall in no manner lend its support to this third party.

   Article III. The Governments of the two High Contracting Parties shall in the future maintain continual contact with one another for the purpose of consultation in order to exchange
15 information on problems affecting their common interest. . . .

   Article V. Should disputes or conflicts arise between the High Contracting Parties, both Parties shall settle these disputes exclu-

sively through friendly exchange of opinion, or, if necessary, through the establishment of arbitration commissions.
20   Article VI. The present treaty is concluded for a period of ten years . . .
Secret Additional protocol
1 In the event of a territorial and political arrangement in the areas belonging to the Baltic States (Finland, Estonia, Latvia,
25 Lithuania), the northern boundary of Lithuania shall represent the boundary of the spheres of influence of Germany and the USSR . . .
2 The question of whether the interests of both parties make desirable the maintenance of an independent Polish state and how
30 such a state should be bounded can only be definitely determined in the course of further developments.

*At the beginning of September 1939, German forces began to occupy Poland. Four weeks later, under the terms of the Pact, Germany and the USSR signed a formal agreement dividing Poland between them:

1 28th Sept, 1939
The Government of the German Reich and the Government of the USSR consider it as exclusively their task, after the collapse of the former Polish state, to re-establish peace and order in these
5 territories. To this end they have agreed upon the following:
The Government of the German Reich and the Government of the USSR shall determine the boundary of their respective national interests in the territory of the former Polish state . . .
The territory of the Lithuanian state falls into the sphere of
10 influence of the USSR, while the province of Lublin, and parts of the province of Warsaw fall to the influence of Germany . . . Both Parties will tolerate in their territories no Polish agitation which affects the territories of the other Party. They will suppress in their territories all beginnings of such agitation and inform each
15 other concerning suitable measures.

*The Nazi–Soviet Pact staggered the rest of the world. The impossible had occurred; the sworn ideological enemies, Nazi Germany and Communist Russia, had come together. But there was a logic to this remarkable change in Soviet foreign policy. Stalin had been left with no alternative, given the very real threat that Germany presented and the indifference of Paris and London to his offers of a Soviet defence alliance. He had acted on the axiom 'if you can't beat them, join them', and had attempted to nullify the danger from Germany by the only move that international circumstances still allowed.

'Rendezvous' (A David Low cartoon in the Daily Express, *September 1939)*

The fruits of the Pact were gathered during the next two years. The USSR duly seized the eastern half of Poland. Germany was free to conduct its war against France and Britain in the west, while in the east the USSR added to its Polish prize by forcibly taking hold of the Baltic states, southern Finland, and Bessarabia-Bukovina (see map on page 83). By 1941 Soviet Russia had regained all the territories it had lost as a result of the First World War. All this, added to the ten-year guarantee of peace with Germany, seemed to justify the praise heaped on Stalin inside the Soviet Union for his diplomatic master-stroke.

The extravagant claim made for the Nazi-Soviet Pact was that it had safeguarded Soviet security by a guarantee of freedom from western attack, and had thus fulfilled the chief objective for which Soviet foreign policy had been struggling since the days of Lenin. Stalin appears to have believed his own propaganda. It is one of the inexplicable things about him that he remained blind to the fact that Hitler's clear intention was to invade and occupy Russia. An outstanding and consistent feature of Nazism from its beginnings had been its ideological conviction that Germany had a providential destiny to expand eastwards at the expense of the Slav lands, including Russia. Between August 1939 and June 1941 Stalin chose to ignore this. It is also highly curious that he failed to realise that the Pact, which gave Germany a free hand in the war which broke out in Western Europe in September 1939, made the German invasion of Russia likely to come

SOVIET EXPANSION
1939–49

Miles
0   100

0   100
Km

FINLAND

Viborg
Leningrad

DENMARK

SWEDEN

ESTONIA

LATVIA

LITHUANIA

HOLLAND

1949
Berlin

E. GERMANY

1947
POLAND

FRANCE

W. GERMANY

1948

CZECHOSLOVAKIA

SWITZERLAND

AUSTRIA

1947
HUNGARY

BB

1948
RUMANIA

ITALY

YUGOSLAVIA

ALBANIA

GREECE

BULGARIA
1948

Key

Annexed by USSR, 1939–41

Areas falling under Soviet control post-war (with dates)

BB   Bessarabia-Bukovina

the Iron Curtain

sooner rather than later. The fall of France in June 1940, and the inability of Britain to do more than survive, encouraged Hitler to launch his long-intended attack upon the USSR in June 1941.

*Operation Barbarossa, as the invasion of Russia was code-named by Hitler, was on a huge scale and the preparations for it could not be hidden. For many months before it was unleashed the USSR had known of its likelihood. Yet still Stalin did nothing. Perhaps it was that he could not bring himself to admit that the Nazi–Soviet Pact had proved a failure. Perhaps he genuinely believed that Hitler could still be bought off. This would explain why, in 1941, he offered more and more Soviet military and economic concessions to Germany. However mysterious his reasoning, the outcome of it was clear enough. Because he was unwilling to admit the reality of the situation in June 1941 none of his underlings could take the initiative. The result was that in the first few days of the Second World War on the eastern front the German forces overran a Soviet Union that was wholly without effective leadership and direction.

6 The Grand Alliance, 1941–45

Stalin's subsequent rapid recovery of nerve and his resolute and inspiring leadership of the USSR through four long years of bitter attrition to eventual victory in 1945 was portrayed in Soviet propaganda as a great anti-fascist crusade. However, the truth was that Stalin had not entered the war against Germany willingly. The object of Stalin's policy, before 1941, had been to reach a compromise with Nazism, not fight against it. This had an important bearing on the nature of Stalin's relations with the USSR's principal wartime allies, Britain and the USA. The three countries became allies not through choice, but through circumstance. The Soviet Union had made no effort to assist Britain in her struggle with Germany between 1939 and 1941. The USA had no thought of helping the USSR until December 1941 when, following Pearl Harbour, Germany, as an ally of Japan, declared war on the United States. The coming together of the 'Big Three', the Soviet Union, the USA and Britain, became known as 'the Grand Alliance'. However, a more accurate description might be 'the marriage of convenience'. What bound them together was their desire to defeat the common enemy. They had little else in common. In public frequent tributes were made to the war efforts of their glorious allies, but behind the scenes there was constant bickering between the Soviet Union and her two Western partners.

A major irritant was the question of a second front. From the beginning of the alliance Stalin pleaded with the other allies to create a second military front against Germany in occupied Europe in order to take the strain off the USSR, which was bearing the brunt of the fighting. Britain's response was to promise that when sufficient forces and supplies were available a second front would be started, but also to argue that to engage in a premature invasion of Europe would be suicidal folly. Stalin retorted that neither Britain nor the USA truly understood the intensity of the war to the death on the eastern front, and that their caution was at the expense of the Russian dead. When Churchill referred to the opening of allied fronts in North Africa Stalin taunted him by asking whether British troops were afraid to fight Germans. Churchill reacted by asking Stalin whether he had forgotten the bravery and sacrifice of the Royal and Merchant Navies in keeping the Soviet Union supplied with essential war materials from Britain and the USA.

*These taunts and recriminations did not prevent personal contact being maintained between the leaders of the allies, but they did indicate the lack of true understanding between them. As the war drew towards its end and the defeat of Germany became increasingly probable, the ideological differences between the USSR and the other allies, which had been largely submerged because of the need for wartime co-operation, began to resurface. There was fear in the Soviet Union that Britain and the USA would show their true capitalist colours by attempting to enlist Germany in a war against Soviet Communism. On the Western side, there was anxiety that the Soviet advance into eastern Europe and Germany heralded the start of a new period of Communist expansion.

Therefore, when Stalin, Churchill and Roosevelt met at Yalta in February 1945 to plan the post-war settlement, there was great tension behind the official cordiality. As a result, the agreements they reached were temporary compromises that did not settle the larger issues. On the question of the treatment of defeated Germany, it was agreed that the country would be divided into four zones, to be separately administered by the USA, the USSR, France and Britain, but there was no common understanding on a uniform system of government in the zones. Attempts to arrive at agreement on the scale of the German payment of war reparations proved equally fruitless. In the event, it was impossible to reconcile Stalin's demand, that the 20 million Russian war-dead merited the harshest economic penalties being imposed on Germany, with the Western allies' determination not to allow Russia to drain Germany dry while they were pouring in resources to prevent the country's collapse. Stalin was later to claim, in the face of Western denials, that Yalta had guaranteed the USSR 50% of German reparations.

Among the most significant of the issues discussed at Yalta was the settlement of Poland. As a result of the war, the USSR had occupied Poland and had installed a pro-Soviet Provisional Government, with the promise of future democratic elections. Britain and the USA did not trust Stalin, and feared that Poland would simply become a Soviet puppet. However, the presence of the Red Army in Poland and the readiness of the Western allies to appease Stalin on some issues in order to gain concessions elsewhere led Churchill reluctantly to grant Stalin's wishes. The same considerations generally applied to most of eastern and central Europe, which had been occupied by the Red Army in the later stages of the war. A joint 'Allied Declaration on Liberated Europe' formally committed the USSR to pursue a policy of democracy in those areas it now occupied, but Stalin's interpretation of democracy was very different from that of the other allies. The position that Stalin took was a simple one. He was determined to create a large buffer against any future German aggression, which he now equated with Western anti-Communism. He was not prepared to withdraw Soviet forces from the countries of eastern Europe until pro-Soviet governments had been installed. 'What we have, we hold', was Stalin's unyielding position. Eastern Europe would have to pay the price for Soviet security.

The differences that emerged between the powers over Poland and eastern Europe weakened such agreements as were reached at Yalta. There was deep suspicion between East and West. This was indicated by Stalin's hesitation in bringing the USSR into the United Nations Organisation, the international body that replaced the League of Nations as a result of the Yalta agreement. It was fear of being out-numbered by the capitalist powers that led to his insistence, as a condition of Russia's joining, on the right of the single-member veto in the proposed five-nation UN Security Council, made up of the four occupying powers of Europe plus Chiang Kai-shek's China.

*At Yalta, the general expectation was that the Japanese war would continue for a number of years. It was in the light of this that Stalin did a secret deal with Roosevelt. In return for the USSR's entering the war to assist the USA, large areas of Chinese territory would be ceded to it after Japan had been defeated. Stalin struck a hard bargain. Later critics of Roosevelt suggested that his acceptance of Stalin's territorial demands in the Far East was an act of appeasement equivalent to Churchill's over Poland. Ironically, the USA was to have no need of Soviet help in the war against Japan. The break-through in the American development of the atomic bomb came in July, and its use against Japan in August occasioned a swift and dramatic end to the Pacific war. This did not prevent Stalin's keeping to the letter of the original agreement. The USSR declared war on Japan in the brief time between the dropping of the two atomic bombs and the Japanese surrender. Stalin duly proceeded to claim the Soviet Union's territorial rewards in the Far East.

The Potsdam Conference that began in July 1945 was essentially a continuation of Yalta. The issues under discussion – Germany, reparations, eastern Europe, Japan – were the same, and produced the same antipathy between the Soviet Union and the other allies. The short period between the two conferences appeared to have worsened relations. The Reparations Commission, established at Yalta, had produced no acceptable settlement in regard to German war debts, and Soviet ruthlessness in Poland and eastern Europe suggested that Stalin was intent on imposing as rigid a system there as prevailed in the USSR itself. Stalin's attitude at Potsdam was even more uncompromising than it had been at Yalta. He was not prepared to concede on any of the major issues. He was strengthened in this by the fact that he was undoubtedly the dominant statesman at the Conference. Both the USA and Britain had new leaders, Truman and Attlee respectively, whereas Stalin had attended both conferences. Such continuity worked to his advantage in negotiations. Even the news, which Truman gave him during the Potsdam Conference, of the USA's successful detonation of the world's first atom bomb did not shake Stalin from his strong diplomatic position. If anything, it made him still more determined to safeguard the USSR's recently acquired gains in Europe. The concessions over Poland and eastern Europe that he had extracted from Britain and the USA at the Yalta Conference remained substantially unaltered.

7 The Cold War

Yalta and Potsdam were not so much international agreements as recognitions by the Western powers of the *de facto* extension of Soviet power in Europe. In that sense they were definitions of the new international balance, known as the Cold War. This is best understood as the period, beginning in 1945 and outlasting Stalin, during which the Communist world, led by the Soviet Union, faced its great ideological enemy, the United States and her capitalist allies, in a prolonged test of nerve. Many commentators have emphasised Stalin's refusal to consider German reunification or to give up the USSR's wartime gains in eastern Europe as a major factor in creating the Cold War. It has also frequently been suggested that Stalin never fully understood the Western position. While this is true, it is not the whole story. The misunderstanding was two-way. There was a Soviet perspective that the West never genuinely appreciated. Despite her victory over Germany and the emergence of Stalin as an outstanding world statesman, the Soviet Union felt more vulnerable than at any time since the Revolution. It was a matter of economics. Whatever advances had been made under Stalin, the strain of total war from 1941 to 1945 had exhausted the Russian economy; this was one reason why Stalin had been so adamant at Yalta on the issue of German reparations. The fear that he had always had of the West's being able to swamp the USSR was intensified by his knowledge of the USA's capacity, as witnessed by her prodigious war effort and the construction of the atomic bomb. The traditional Soviet claim to possess an intrinsically superior economic and cultural system would be hard to sustain in the face of post-1945 international realities.

Since the USSR could not hope to compete on equal economic terms with the USA, Stalin calculated that the only policy available to him after 1945 was to withdraw the Soviet Union behind its new defensive barrier, provided by the wartime acquisition of eastern Europe. Germany became the new front line in this defensive system, which explains why Stalin became so sensitive and uncooperative on the German question, always regarding Western suggestions for a settlement as the thin end of a wedge being driven into Soviet security. This was well illustrated by the issue of West Berlin. The post-war settlement had created a political anomaly by leaving the western part of the East-German capital isolated as a capitalist enclave within Communist Europe. In 1948 Stalin instructed the East Germans to blockade West Berlin. This was not, as the Western nations thought, a mere act of hostility; it was a desperate attempt to end the affront to Soviet security of a Western outpost 100 miles inside Soviet-controlled East Germany.

*In the atmosphere of the Cold War, the West misinterpreted Soviet defensive moves as a desire for expansion. The abiding anxiety of the USA after 1945 was that Europe, enfeebled by war, would easily fall prey to a politically and economically aggressive Soviet Union. To avoid this and so prevent the crises in the international economy that had occurred after the First World War, in 1947 the United States introduced the Marshall Aid Plan, which offered large amounts of American capital to enable the nations of Europe to undertake postwar economic reconstruction. The Western European nations accepted the Plan, and their recovery began. The USA's intention was expressed by General Marshall when he introduced his Plan in June 1947:

1 Our policy is directed not against any country or doctrine but against hunger, poverty, desperation, and chaos. Its purpose should be the revival of a working economy in the world, so as to permit the emergence of political and social conditions in which
5 free institutions can exist.

That was not how the Soviets saw it. They condemned the Plan as a thin cover for American imperialism. They linked it with the recently promulgated Truman Doctrine. In 1947 an over-burdened Britain had declared her intention to withdraw her forces from Greece and Turkey. Fearing that this would leave those two countries at the mercy of the USSR, as had occurred throughout the Balkans, the USA made a momentous decision. President Truman promised that America would now undertake the defence of Greece and Turkey. More significant still, he announced that the USA regarded it as her duty to give active support to free peoples resisting attempted subjugation. The USSR was not expressly named as the aggressor, but Truman pointedly referred to a world divided between democracy and totalitarianism. The implica-

tion could not have been clearer. Coming so soon after the promulga-
tion of the Truman Doctrine, the Marshall Plan seemed to the Soviet
Union to be deliberately linked with it. Stalin's bitter reaction was
angrily voiced by the Soviet representative at the UN:

1 As is now clear, the Marshall Plan constitutes in essence merely a
variant of the Truman Doctrine, adapted to the conditions of
post-war Europe. It is becoming more and more evident that the
implementation of the Marshall Plan will mean placing European
5 countries under the economic and political control of the United
States and direct interference by the latter in the internal affairs of
those countries. Moreover, this plan is an attempt to split Europe
into two camps and to complete the formation of a bloc of several
European countries hostile to the interests of the democratic
10 countries of Eastern Europe and most particularly to the Soviet
Union.
   An important feature of this Plan is the attempt to confront the
countries of Eastern Europe with a bloc of Western European
States, including Western Germany. The intention is to make use
15 of Western Germany and German heavy industry (the Ruhr) as
one of the most important economic bases for American expansion in Europe, in disregard of the national interests of the
countries which suffered from German aggression.
(from a speech by A. Vyshinsky to the UN General Assembly,
20   September 1947)

*If the announcement of the Marshall Plan had preceded rather than
followed the issuing of the Truman Doctrine, there might have been a
chance of the Soviet Union's accepting its good faith. This in turn
might have prevented the hardening of the Cold War. The USSR's
economic plight made Marshall Aid a sorely tempting offer, and Stalin
for a brief period considered accepting it. But in the end, as Vyshinsky's speech illustrated, he felt that he could not risk allowing the
Eastern bloc to become economically dependent upon the United
States. The political dangers were too great. It is arguable also that Cold
War suspicions rendered an economic arrangement between East and
West no longer feasible. Distrust of the intentions of the USA was
further justified in Soviet eyes by the formation of NATO in 1949. In
the West this was represented as a defensive alliance, freely entered into
by the nations of Western Europe and North America for their greater
mutual protection. To the Soviet Union it was a further stage in the
spread of American militarism and imperialism, begun by the Truman
Doctrine and Marshall Plan. It justified the USSR's responding in kind
by building a military alliance in the Eastern bloc and it proved the
wisdom of Stalin's 1945 decision to develop the Soviet Union's own
atomic weapon.

*Relations between the USA and the USSR were not eased by their contacts in the United Nations. Indeed, in some respects their membership of the UN intensified their disputes. Both the General Assembly, in which all member-states were represented, and the Security Council, the permanent five-member body responsible for settling international disputes, provided platforms for propaganda and point-scoring. In the Security Council, discussion of the major international problems of the post-war world – Persia, Greece, Germany, Korea – became a constant battleground between the USSR, regularly using its veto, and the non-Communist members. Outnumbered as it was, Soviet Russia did not view the veto as a last resort but as the instrument for redressing the anti-Soviet imbalance of the Security Council. The strains between the USSR and the USA in the UN were at their most severe over China. The victory of the Communists there, in 1949, led to the Soviet proposal that Mao's new China be recognised and admitted to the UN in place of Chiang's American-backed, Nationalist China. The failure of this proposal led the Soviet delegation to stage a protest walk-out from the Security Council. This gesture rebounded against the USSR. While the Soviet delegation was absent, the Council, free of the inevitable Soviet veto, was able to pass a resolution setting up a UN army to defend South Korea against the Communist invasion from the North. The first open military conflict of the Cold War had begun.

Although the Soviet Union was not involved militarily in Korea, the war there from 1950 to 1953 was the dominant international issue during the last three years of Stalin's life. He gave the North Koreans and the Chinese Communists the diplomatic backing of the USSR. When he died in 1953 his country was locked in an implacable ideological struggle with the capitalist West. This was the same situation that he had inherited in 1924.

*Stalin's foreign policy was sometimes complex in its operation, but it was essentially simple in its design. He set himself the primary task of defending his country's interests in a hostile world. Having, in any practical sense, abandoned the notion of the USSR leading an international Marxist revolution, he settled for the less ambitious but equally demanding task of safeguarding national security. He never lost his deep fear of a Western invasion. No matter how powerful he and the Soviet Union became, Stalin never ceased to regard the Soviet Union as vulnerable. That is the explanation for his decision to opt for 'socialism in one country'. His domestic policies were never an end in themselves; they had to serve the needs of national defence. His often-repeated warning that unless the Soviet Union modernised 'they will crush us' was the simple expression of this. The irony was that when the invasion he dreaded did actually come he refused to believe it. He was at his least ready when he should have been at his most prepared. The German invasion of 1941 very nearly destroyed all that Stalin had achieved since 1929. The manner of the Soviet Union's eventual military recovery by

1945 exhausted the country economically, but at the same time made the USSR undeniably a world power and Stalin a world statesman. This, however, did not lessen his sense of vulnerability. Whatever the various causes of the Cold War, they were in part the product of Stalin's determination never to be caught out again. His refusal to contemplate the reunification of Germany or the freedom of Eastern Europe followed from this. His suspicion of the outside world in the post-war years created an atmosphere of bitterness and distrust, which conditioned Western attitudes towards the USSR and shaped the Soviet Union's perception of itself.

Making Notes on 'Stalin and International Relations'

Your notes on this chapter should provide you with an outline of Stalin's foreign policy over the whole of his period of power. With such a large area to cover, it is important that you do not get lost in detail. Your aim should be to provide yourself with enough material to understand the principles and motives behind his policy. The following headings, sub-headings and questions should help you:

1 **Background**
1.1 What basic problems faced the Bolsheviks in their approach to foreign relations after 1917? The importance of Rapallo.
2 **Soviet Foreign Policy, 1924–29**
2.1 The Zinoviev Letter. The role of the Comintern.
2.2 'Socialism in One Country'. 'Bolshevisation': How did these affect foreign policy? Soviet relations with China and Poland.
3 **Soviet Foreign Policy, 1929–33**
3.1 Stalin's 'Left turn'.
3.2 Why was the USSR unsympathetic to the European Left?
4 **Soviet Foreign Policy, 1933–39**
4.1 The threat of Nazism. USSR advocates 'collective security'.
4.2 Ambiguous Soviet attitudes to the Spanish Civil War.
4.3 How did Stalin interpret the Munich agreement?
5 **The Nazi–Soviet Pact, 1939–41**
5.1 Stalin's motives. Was the Pact a turnabout?
5.2 The USSR's territorial gains.
6 **The Grand Alliance, 1941–45**
6.1 The strains between the allies. 'The marriage of convenience'.
6.2 What did Stalin gain from the Yalta and Potsdam Conferences?
7 **The Cold War**
7.1 The Soviet occupation of eastern Europe. What was Stalin's attitude towards Germany?
7.2 Why did Stalin refuse Marshall Aid? Soviet–American bitterness over China.
7.3 Conclusion.

Answering essay questions on 'Stalin and International Relations'

Foreign affairs cannot be studied in isolation. Internal and external policies interact. To understand Stalin's foreign policy you also need to be familiar with the domestic history of the period, as covered in Chapters 2, 3 and 4.

Examination questions on foreign relations tend to group themselves into two main categories: those dealing with specific events or developments, and those concerned with foreign policy overall. Stalin, of course, is central to all questions, though this does not mean that direct reference is always made to him. It would be useful to make three lists in relation to this theme. Under the headings 'Aims', 'Methods' and 'Style' you will be able to include all the key facts and considerations relevant to Stalin's perception and conduct of Soviet foreign policy.

Consider the following set of questions:

1 How consistent was Soviet foreign policy in the period 1924–1939?
2 'The USSR entered into the 1939 Pact with Nazi Germany not out of choice but out of necessity.' Discuss.
3 How far were Soviet aims achieved at the Yalta and Potsdam Conferences of 1945?
4 To what extent was Stalin personally responsible for the Cold War in international relations after 1945?

Prepare an essay plan for question 1. From your reading of this chapter and the points you have listed in response to the suggestions in the *Making Notes* section, you will appreciate that fundamental to all four questions is the matter of Stalin's objectives. It is not possible to comment convincingly on consistency unless you first establish whether there were any underlying objectives in Soviet foreign policy. This can best be done by drawing on your 'Aims' list to determine what Stalin's objectives were. You should spend the first part of the answer on this aspect, stressing Stalin's basically defensive attitude. With this done, you can then use your 'Methods' list to survey Soviet activities in the period 1924–39 to see how closely Stalin kept to the objectives you have defined. A key point which examiners would expect you to discuss is whether there was a 'turnabout' in Soviet policy in the 1930s. Whether you think there was or not is less important than that you show awareness of the issue. Your conclusion should be a re-statement of Soviet aims and an assessment of how consistently they were pursued.

Using your lists, prepare essay plans for the other three questions. It would be an effective approach in question 2 to explain 'choice' and 'necessity' by reference to Stalin's understanding of the USSR's security needs as they had developed by 1939. 'Choice' suggests options. Did Stalin have any options left in August 1939? In answering that, you are well positioned to answer the set question.

Essay 3 is quite straightforward. State what Stalin's anxieties were in regard to the position of the Soviet Union at the end of the war, and then indicate how he tried to resolve those worries by demanding a post-war territorial settlement that guaranteed Soviet security. Did Yalta and Potsdam provide those guarantees?

The starting point for answering question 4 is similar. How did Stalin perceive the international situation after 1945? His abiding aim of defending the Soviet Union led him to regard his former wartime allies as potential enemies. Did he exaggerate their enmity? Were his fears realistic? How important was his manner as a negotiator and international statesman?

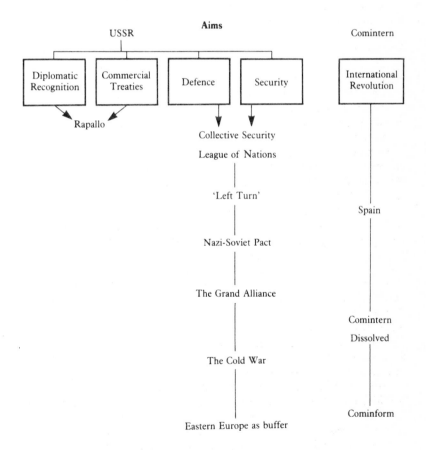

Summary – 'Stalin and International Relations'

Source-based questions on 'Stalin and International Relations'

1 The Zinoviev Letter

Read the extracts from the Zinoviev Letter on page 72 and Baldwin's speech on page 73 and then answer the following questions:

a) According to Zinoviev, what obstacles have to be overcome before the British workers can be turned into a revolutionary force?

b) What are Zinoviev's recommendations for the de-stabilising of the political and military situation in Britain?

c) What points of connection are there between Zinoviev's proposals for revolution and the evidence provided by Baldwin in his speech?

d) The Zinoviev Letter was subsequently shown to be a forgery. Suggest what parties or organisations were likely to have written the letter. What would their motives have been?

e) Why, at the time, were so many people prepared to accept the letter as genuine?

2 The Nazi–Soviet Pact

Read the extracts from the Pact on page 80 and the September agreement on page 81 and study the illustration on page 83 and then answer the following questions:

a) What means of mutual protection for the two Parties are laid down in the Pact?

b) What provisions does the Pact contain for preventing or resolving future disputes between the two Parties?

c) In what ways does the 'Secret Additional Protocol' prepare the ground for the division of Poland, as referred to in the September agreement?

d) How does Low's cartoon illustrate the bewilderment and anger of the Western world over the Nazi–Soviet Pact?

e) What features of the Nazi–Soviet Pact may have suggested to Stalin that it represented a lasting settlement of Soviet–German differences?

3 The Marshall Plan

Read the extract from General Marshall's speech on page 88 and the extract from Vyshinsky's speech at the UN on page 89 and then answer the following questions:

a) Marshall speaks (in line 3) of 'the revival of a working economy in the world'. On what grounds does Vyshinsky in his speech reject this concept?

b) Explain what Vyshinsky means by describing the Marshall Plan as 'merely a variant of the Truman Doctrine' (line 1).

c) What Soviet fears lie behind Vyshinsky's charge that 'this Plan is the attempt to split Europe into two camps' (line 7)?

d) In what respects is Vyshinsky's speech an expression of Stalin's Cold War attitudes?

CHAPTER 6

Khrushchev

1 Early Career

Nikita Khrushchev was born in 1894 into a poor peasant family in Kalnikova, a small town in southern Russia, close to the Ukrainian border. He received little formal education and at the age of 15 he left the land to become an apprentice fitter in the mining industry. His value as a worker is suggested by his exemption from military duty in the 1914–17 war. He did, however, see active service soon after. Having joined the Bolshevik Party in 1918, he became a Red Army commissar during the Civil War. Throughout the 1920s he was active in Ukrainian affairs, serving as the Party's district secretary in a number of areas, including Kiev, the capital. In the 1930s he began to climb the Party ladder. He moved to Moscow and was appointed a district secretary there in 1931. By 1935 he had become the Party Secretary for the whole capital. Khrushchev's elevation has to be set against the background of the purges. As with all who rose within the Party or government in this period, Khrushchev was stepping into disgraced men's, often dead men's, shoes. The price of political survival was unswerving loyalty to Stalin, and Khrushchev was exemplary in this respect. For the next three years he played his part in the continuing purge of suspected anti-Stalinists in Moscow. At the end of 1938 he went back to the Ukraine as First Party Secretary to carry out similar work there. His reward was to be made a member of the Politburo in the following year. In the war years, 1941–45, during which large parts of the Ukraine suffered German occupation, he was a political commissar in the army, involved in organising military and civilian resistance. He fought at Stalingrad and was among the Soviet forces that liberated Kiev.

Immediately after the war Khrushchev returned as First Party Secretary in the Ukraine. Despite a short and obscure period in 1948 when he was suspended from office, he remained unwavering in his commitment to Stalin, frequently eulogising him in the manner required of public officials. An extract from one of Khrushchev's speeches to the Ukrainian Communist Party in 1949 suggests the character of this:

1 All our successes we owe to the great Bolshevik Party and to the experienced guidance of our beloved leader and teacher, Comrade Stalin. Millions of workers in all countries of the world see how the Soviet Union is carrying out the great socialist ideas, the ideas
5 of Marx–Engels–Lenin–Stalin.

In 1949 Khrushchev was summoned to Moscow by Stalin. He was

appointed Secretary to the General Committee and given particular responsibility for the planning of Soviet agriculture, an extension of the specialism he had developed as an administrator in the Ukraine. His work was not an outstanding success. One of his schemes for developing agricultural centres in the countryside, known as 'agro-towns', failed to materialise and he was derided in *Pravda*. Such lack of success did not suggest that he was destined for leadership. At the time of Stalin's death in 1953 Khrushchev was an industrious but not politically outstanding member of the Politburo. His breezy, talkative manner made him appear less devious and scheming than the usual Bolshevik politicians. His colleagues tended to underrate his ambition and his ruthlessness.

2 Rise to Power

There are interesting parallels between Stalin's coming to power in the 1920s and Khrushchev's in the 1950s. Both Lenin and Stalin had failed to make any clear provision for the succession. After each one's death there was a period of collective leadership which turned into a power struggle, resulting in both instances in the victory of the least regarded or likely individual.

Kremlin power struggles have never been easy for the outsider to disentangle, but enough evidence has come to light to provide a reasonably reliable narrative. Following Stalin's death in March 1953, the collective leadership that emerged was made up of Malenkov (Soviet Premier), Molotov (Foreign Secretary), Bulganin (Deputy Premier), and Khrushchev (Party Secretary). Their initial anxiety was that Lavrenti Beria, Stalin's chief of the MVD (successor organisation to the NKVD) might attempt to use the secret police apparatus as a base for a power bid. The MVD certainly represented a major force in the Soviet Union, but Khrushchev was able to counter-balance it with the Red Army. The generals disliked Beria for his role in the Great Purge of the armed forces in the 1930s, but they felt that Khrushchev's war record gave him a special authority; he alone of the collective leaders had actually fought in the Great Patriotic Struggle. The Soviet Commander-in-Chief, Marshal Zhukov, especially admired Khrushchev. It was on the strength of this that Khrushchev was able to enlist the army's support. In June 1953 a contingent of troops surrounded Beria's apartment, blocking any possibility of the MVD preventing his arrest. He was taken into custody, summarily tried and shot. This was one of the few executions during the post-Stalin power struggle. In the future the penalty for political defeat would be demotion or dismissal. The blood-lettings of the 1920s and 1930s were not to be repeated. This may be seen as one aspect of 'the thaw', the relative easing of tension and restrictions, that set in following Stalin's death.

*It was due as much to Malenkov, the Premier, as anyone that 'the thaw' had begun. He had argued the need for better relations with the outside world and had suggested that attention be given to the raising of Soviet standards of living at the expense of investment in heavy industry. However, his progressive thinking brought him no political benefits. Despite the fact that he had been tipped by many to become the next leader, he found himself outmanoeuvred by Khrushchev. One basic problem for him was that, although he was an able administrator, he was no match for Khrushchev in strength of personality. He lacked Khrushchev's forcefulness and power of persuasion. Another difficulty for him, not dissimilar to that which had faced the competitors to Stalin after 1924, was that Khrushchev was much better placed than he to sustain a power bid. Malenkov, as Premier, was head of government. Khrushchev, as First Secretary, was the effective head of the Party. This enabled Khrushchev over the next two years to undermine Malenkov's position in the Soviet system. He did not do this by open attack but by using his influence with Party members to criticise government policies, ministers and officials. He travelled widely about the countryside (something seldom done by Russian leaders, either before or after the Revolution), listening to complaints and making personal contact with a wide range of people and officials. It was a custom he continued after he came to power. He placed his own nominees in positions of authority, as Stalin had done, and began to establish a power base. By 1955 he was undoubtedly the dominant member of the collective leadership that had succeeded Stalin. It was in that year that Malenkov, publicly admitting that he was to blame for the current shortfall in grain production, resigned his premiership, and gave up any thought of further contending for power. He was replaced by Bulganin. For some time Bulganin and Khrushchev exercised what in appearance was a joint authority, but in reality Bulganin was very much the subordinate.

*By 1956 Khrushchev felt strong enough to launch a withering attack upon Stalin's character and record. This destruction of the Stalin legend staggered Party officials and made them fear for the future because, in one obvious sense, they were all Stalinists. Undeniably, they had all survived to hold their current positions because they had participated in, and benefited from, Stalin's terror. Many of them found it difficult to adapt to life without Stalin. They were perplexed and frightened by the implications of Khrushchev's attack upon him. A line from a poem of the time expressed their feelings, 'We built upon granite, but now the stone crumbles, dissolves and melts at our feet.' It was around such men that an opposition to Khrushchev began to assemble. This included various disgruntled ministers and officials who had lost their positions as a direct consequence of Khrushchev's policy of decentralisation, aimed at creating greater administrative efficiency.

Throughout Soviet history the main value of the Party to its members had been as a provider of jobs. Anyone interfering with this, as

Khrushchev now was, was bound to arouse opposition. Early in 1957, while he was temporarily absent on one of his many visits abroad, the opposition made plans to remove him. Soon after his return, he had to face a concerted attack. Declaring that de-Stalinisation had gone too far and had been responsible for the recent anti-Soviet revolts in Poland and Hungary [see page 103], the Politburo voted by seven to four for his dismissal as Party Secretary. Khrushchev proved equal to the challenge. He refused to accept the Politburo's decision unless it was backed by a vote of the full Central Committee of the Party. Using his good offices with the army, he arranged to have his own supporters specially flown in from various parts of the USSR to attend the Moscow meeting. The gamble worked. The Central Committee voted to overrule the Politburo's decision. Molotov, Kaganovich and Malenkov were then censured for having formed an 'anti-Party Group'. They duly resigned from their ministerial posts.

*Having previously turned to the army as a saviour, Khrushchev now took steps to prevent its becoming a threat. Playing upon internal jealousies within the high command, he undermined the position of his long-standing supporter, Marshall Zhukov, who was accused of creating his own 'cult of the individual'. Zhukov was forced to retire, to be replaced by Marshall Malinovsky as Commander-in-Chief. It only remained to demote Bulganin, which Khrushchev did by inducing him to confess to being implicated with the 'anti-Party Group'. In March 1958 Bulganin resigned as Premier and lost his place on the Central Committee. Shortly after, Khrushchev took over that post himself. For the first time since Stalin's death, five years earlier, one man held the offices of Prime Minister in the government and First Secretary in the Party. As later events were to show, this did not give Khrushchev absolute power. He remained answerable to the Politburo and Central Committee in a way that Stalin had not been. But for the next six years he was the pre-eminent Soviet figure, both as a domestic leader and as a world statesman.

3 De-Stalinisation

The process of destroying Stalin's reputation began dramatically with Khrushchev's 'secret report' to the Twentieth Congress of the CPSU in February 1956. Some signs had already appeared between 1953 and 1956 to suggest that Stalin's record might be reappraised by the new leaders of the Soviet Union. References in the press to his greatness and omniscience became less frequent and the changes in policy introduced by Malenkov were an implied criticism of Stalin's strategies. However, what was totally unexpected was the range and venom of Khrushchev's attack. In his report, which took a whole weekend to deliver, Khrushchev surveyed Stalin's career since the 1930s, exposing in detail the errors and crimes that Stalin had committed against the Party. Stalin

*A Soviet cartoon from the period of collective leadership after Stalin's death.
An official is given a dose of 'criticism'. The label on the bottle says it is a
cure for 'gullibility, complacency, twaddle, conceit, bureaucratism and other
ailments'.*

had been guilty of 'flagrant abuses of power'. He had been personally
responsible for the purges, 'those mass arrests that brought tremendous
harm to our country and to the cause of socialist progress'. Khrushchev
quoted a host of names of innocent Party members who had suffered at
Stalin's hands. Individual cases of gross injustice were cited and
examples given of the brutality and torture used to extract confessions.
Khrushchev's address was frequently interrupted by outbursts of
amazement and disbelief from the assembled members as he gave the
details of the Stalinist terror. Although Khrushchev's report was
known as 'the secret speech', within days the foreign Communists who
had attended the Congress had leaked the details to the Western press
and translations appeared worldwide. These provided a vivid picture of
Khrushchev's speech and the response it occasioned:

1 Of the 139 members and candidates of the Party Central Committee who were elected at the Seventeenth Congress, 98 persons, ie
  70%, were shot, mostly in 1937–8. (*Indignation in the hall*) The
  only reason why this 70% were branded enemies of the Party and
5 of the people was that honest Communists were slandered,
  accusations against them were fabricated, and revolutionary
  legality was gravely undermined. (*Gasps from members*)
  The same fate befell not only the Central Committee members

but also the majority of the delegates to the Seventeenth Party
10 Congress. Of 1966 delegates, 1108 persons were arrested on
charges of counter-revolutionary crimes. This very fact shows
how absurd, wild and contrary to common sense were the charges
of counter-revolutionary crimes made against a majority of the
participants in the Congress. (*Indignation in the hall*)
15   We should recall that the Seventeenth Party Congress is
historically known as the Congress of the Victors. Delegates to
the Congress were active participants in the building of our
socialist state; many of them fought and suffered for Party
interests during the revolutionary years and at the Civil War
20 fronts. How then can we believe that such people could prove to
be 'two-faced' and join the camp of the enemies of socialism
during the era of the liquidation of the Zinovievites, Trotskyites
and Rightists and after the great accomplishments of socialist
construction? (*Prolonged applause from members*)
25   An example of vile provocation, of odious falsification, and of
criminal violation of revolutionary legality is the case of the
former candidate member of the Central Committee, Comrade
Eikhe, who had been a Party member since 1905. (*Commotion in
the hall*) Eikhe was arrested 29 April 1938, on the basis of
30 slanderous materials. He was forced under torture to sign a
confession in which he and several other eminent Party workers
were accused of anti-Soviet activity. Comrade Eikhe was shot 4
February. (*Indignation in the hall*) It has been definitely established now that Eikhe's case was fabricated. He has been
35 posthumously rehabilitated. (*Applause from members*)

*Khrushchev did not limit himself to the purges in his denunciation
of Stalin. He attacked him for his failures in foreign policy, particularly
with regard to the Eastern-bloc countries. He also ridiculed the idea of
Stalin as a war hero, pointing out his incompetence as an organiser and
strategist; one of Khrushchev's jibes was that Stalin had used a globe
rather than a detailed map by which to plan the defence of the Soviet
Union. The special term that Khrushchev used to describe the
Stalinism that he was condemning was 'the cult of personality'. He
explained that he meant by this that all the mistakes perpetrated in the
Soviet Union since the 1930s had been a consequence of Stalin's lust for
personal power, his 'mania for greatness'.
    It is significant that although Khrushchev read out a long list of
Stalin's victims who were now to be officially pardoned, it did not go
back before 1934 and did not include such names as Trotsky or
Bukharin. Khrushchev's list was a selective one. His purpose was to
blacken Stalin's name, not to criticise the Communist Party. It was
important that the illegality and terror he was exposing should be seen

as the crimes of one individual. In theory and in practice the Party was the essential power base in the Soviet system, and Khrushchev was anxious not to challenge the justification for his own authority.

By any measure Khrushchev's 'secret' speech was a remarkable event in Soviet and Communist history. For a quarter of a century before 1953 Stalin had exercised astonishing power. Having destroyed his opponents, he had assumed an unchallengeable leadership. Revered as the heir to Lenin, Stalin had become the voice of Communism itself. Therefore, to attack such a legend so soon after Stalin's death raised the very real possibility of disruption within the Soviet Union and in the ranks of international Communism. Why, then, did Khrushchev decide on this hazardous move?

De-Stalinisation had three basic aims: to justify the introduction of more progressive economic measures within the USSR, to help towards co-existence with the West and to absolve Khrushchev and the other current Soviet leaders from their complicity in Stalin's errors. This last aim was of particular importance; criticism of Stalin personally was the only way to explain the otherwise inexplicable failures of the Soviet system during the post-Lenin era. Khrushchev was taking a risk in undermining Stalin's reputation. He knew that he was laying himself open to the charge of having been an accessory to the offences that he was now condemning. After all, he had helped carry out the purges in Moscow and the Ukraine. But Khrushchev calculated that, since all the Soviet leaders had climbed to their present positions by carrying out Stalin's orders, none of them had an entirely clean record. Khrushchev estimated that this common guilt would prevent any serious challenge being offered to his denunciation of Stalin.

*At the time, the peoples of the Soviet satellites and many observers in the West interpreted these developments as signs that the USSR was moving towards tolerance and freedom. They were mistaken. De-Stalinisation was never intended to be a genuine liberalising of Soviet society. It is true that large numbers of political prisoners were released from the labour camps which had proliferated under Stalin and that there was some lifting of State censorship, but these were gestures rather than a wholesale abandonment of Soviet totalitarianism. It is significant in this context that at no time during this period was Stalin attacked for his terrorising of the Soviet people. The charge against him was always expressed in terms of crimes against the Party. The logic of Khrushchev's concentrating his attack on Stalin's 'cult of personality' was that it reduced the responsibility for the errors of the past to one man. The reputation and authority of the Party was thereby undiminished. This left the new leaders of the Party free to introduce changes of policy and strategy. If Khrushchev was to undertake the reforms that he deemed necessary for the Soviet Union, some form of de-Stalinisation was essential.

4 De-Stalinisation and the Soviet Satellites

Yugoslavia had been the one eastern-European country to have success-fully resisted being brought under Soviet domination in the post-war period. It remained Communist but independent of the USSR. In launching his programme of de-Stalinisation at the Twentieth Party Congress in 1956, Khrushchev made great play of Stalin's mishandling of Tito and the Yugoslav Communists. Khrushchev contended that, had Stalin shown any real understanding of Tito and the national cause he represented, Yugoslavia would never have broken away from the East-European bloc:

1 I recall the first days when the conflict between the Soviet Union
and Yugoslavia began artificially to be blown up. Once, when I
came from Kiev to Moscow, I was invited to visit Stalin, who,
pointing to the copy of a letter lately sent to Tito, asked me 'Have
5 you read this?' Not waiting for my reply, he answered 'I will
shake my little finger and there will be no more Tito. He will fall'.
We have paid dearly for this 'shaking of the little finger'. This
statement reflected Stalin's mania for greatness, but he acted just
that way. 'I will shake my little finger and there will be no more
10 Tito. I will shake my little finger and many others will disappear.'
But this did not happen to Tito. No matter how much or how
little Stalin shook not only his finger but everything else that he
could shake, Tito did not fall. Why? The reason was that in this
case of disagreement with the Yugoslav comrades Tito had
15 behind him a state and a people who had gone through a severe
school of fighting for liberty and independence, a people which
gave support to its leaders.
You see to what Stalin's mania for greatness led? He had
completely lost consciousness of reality; he demonstrated his
20 suspicion and haughtiness not only in relation to individuals in
the USSR, but in relation to whole parties and nations.
We have carefully examined the case of Yugoslavia and have
found a proper solution which is approved by the classes of all the
people's democracies and by all progressive humanity. The
25 liquidation of the abnormal relationship with Yugoslavia was
done in the interest of the whole camp of socialism, in the interest
of strengthening peace in the whole world.

*It is unclear how seriously Khrushchev intended his reference to improved Soviet relations with the socialist camp to be taken. His main purpose appears to have been to illustrate another of Stalin's foreign policy failures. He was not calling for a revision of Eastern-bloc Communism. Nonetheless, that was how many of the Soviet satellites interpreted it. They saw Khrushchev's attack on Stalin over Yugoslavia as an invitation to seek greater national independence themselves. Khrushchev visited Tito in 1955 and 1956. This bestowal of Soviet favour strengthened the idea that, with Stalin gone, the Kremlin had accepted the right of Yugoslavia to develop its own brand of Communism. If this was permissible for Yugoslavia, then why not for the other satellites? Throughout the Eastern bloc there were stirrings of independence. The response was particularly marked in Poland and Hungary. In the former, demands were made for the right of Poland to advance its own form of socialism. Facing mounting pressure, Khrushchev and the Kremlin leaders compromised for a time by allowing the popular Polish patriot, Gomulka, who had been outlawed in Stalin's day, to return to political prominence. However, Gomulka was required to promise to discourage 'revisionism' in Poland and to renew the commitment of his country to the Warsaw Pact.

How determined the USSR under Khrushchev was to prevent the loosening of the Soviet grip was clearly revealed in its reaction to events in Hungary in 1956. In its early stages the Hungarian 'thaw' seemed to be acceptable to Moscow. Imre Nagy who, like Gomulka, had been denied public office during the Stalin years, was allowed to return as the new Hungarian leader. Appearances were deceptive. When the Nagy government began to tolerate, if not encourage, anti-Soviet popular demonstrations, Khrushchev decided things had gone too far. Disturbed by Western attempts to raise the Hungarian independence issue in the UN, by the declared intention of the Budapest Government to open politics to non-Communists and, most disturbing of all, by Nagy's desire to withdraw his country from the Warsaw Pact, the Kremlin ordered the long-threatened invasion. Russian tanks entered Budapest and the Hungarian 'liberal experiment' was crushed.

*Khrushchev's heavy hand in Hungary was clear proof that de-Stalinisation had in no sense been intended as a softening of the USSR's fundamental attitude. When the Soviet Union felt its own security threatened or its control of the Eastern bloc challenged, it was prepared to use the utmost pressure to enforce compliance on its satellites. De-Stalinisation was a false dawn for those who thought it signified genuine independence for Eastern Europe. The reality of the USSR's internal politics, East–West relations, Soviet economic needs and the Soviet Union's claim to leadership of the socialist world meant that post-Stalinist Russia would strengthen, not weaken, its hold over its East–European satellites.

5 Khrushchev and the Soviet Economy

a) Agriculture

It was not long after Stalin's death that the Soviet leaders began to admit that the collectivisation of agriculture had not solved the problem of food production and supply. In 1953 Khrushchev informed the Central Committee that grain stocks under Stalin had been lower than under the last Tsar. Major changes were needed, he argued. Proud of his peasant origins, he justly claimed a special knowledge of agriculture. He made a point of going to meet the peasants in their own localities to discuss their particular problems and needs and to encourage them to adopt more efficient techniques. His broad strategy was to encourage local decision-making. As an incentive to production, the State authorities under Khrushchev's prompting began to pay higher prices to the peasants for their grain; taxes on farming profits were reduced and experts were sent from Moscow to work and advise at local level. The machine tractor stations (MTS) built in Stalin's time were disbanded and turned into repair shops. The tractors themselves were sold to the farmers. The relative success of the incentive scheme can be gauged from the fact that between 1952 and 1958 farm-worker incomes more than doubled. Although wages were still way behind those of industrial workers, prospects of real economic advancement were greater than at any time since the NEP.

*The initiative most closely associated with Khrushchev at this time was the 'virgin lands' policy which was introduced in 1954. This developed into a massive project. Basically the policy aimed at exploiting the previously unused areas of the Soviet Union for crop production. The regions earmarked for particular attention were Kazakhstan and southern Siberia. Over a quarter of a million volunteers, mainly drawn from Komsomol (the Young Communist League), were enlisted to work in these regions. Considerable financial and material investment was put into the scheme, most spectacularly in the provision of 120 000 motorised tractors. Six million acres were freshly ploughed in the virgin lands in the first year of the scheme. There was no doubting the enthusiasm that accompanied the implementation of the policy. Unfortunately, enthusiasm was not enough. It could not make up for the lack of detailed planning. Contrary to Khrushchev's hopes, not enough attention had been paid to local conditions. The good will of the volunteers could not compensate for poor management and short-sighted planning. Crops were often sown in unsuitable soil. Local climatic conditions tended to be ignored. The necessary fertilisers were seldom available in sufficient quantity. In the drive to convert to food stuffs, successful crops such as cotton were replaced by crops such as maize which simply refused to grow. This occurred notably in Kazakhstan where the 'maize mania' often led to whole areas abandoning their traditional planting for the lure of a crop whose yield then proved so poor that it was not worth harvesting. The failure to provide adequate drying and storage facilities frequently meant that such crops as were successfully gathered rotted before they could be distributed. Khrushchev had not been well served by the officials responsible for turning his schemes into reality.

Although there was an increase in Soviet grain production in the 1950s, this was because of greater output in the traditional areas of cultivation rather than in the virgin lands. Official talk of record Soviet harvests, as in 1962, could not disguise the fact that in few areas had production met the set targets. 1963 proved a disastrous year. A combination of poor weather and exhausted, under-fertilised, soil led to a drop of nearly one third in the expected grain output. This created an acute shortage in animal fodder, which in turn led to slaughter and a consequent sharp decrease in livestock. The result was that, in order to avoid what threatened to become a famine, large quantities of North American and Australian grain had to be purchased. What had begun as a grand design to enable the USSR to overtake the Western countries in agricultural production could in the end be sustained only by dependence on supplies from those countries.

b) Industry

There was nothing strikingly original about the industrial policies adopted by Khrushchev. What he did, as in foreign affairs, was to continue the strategies begun by Malenkov before he had been eased out of office. The difference was that Khrushchev applied the policies with a remarkable vigour and enthusiasm. He had what in the West would be classed as a feel for public relations. Khrushchev judged that major changes were called for in the direction of the Soviet economy. He wanted to lessen dependence on heavy industry and give greater prominence to light engineering and chemicals. He was no less insistent on the need for hard work on the part of the population, but, whereas Stalin had used coercion, Khrushchev offered incentives. Stalin's deliberate neglect of consumer goods was replaced by Khrushchev's promise of material rewards. Contemptuous of the huge bureaucracy that had grown up under Stalin, Khrushchev was eager to see the administrative system streamlined and decentralised. His hope was that by transferring economic planning away from the centre the decisions made at local level would prove more realistic and progressive. In reducing central authority, Khrushchev was, of course, upsetting the bureaucratic class. Those many members of the Party who owed their current posts in the governmental and administrative machine to Stalin's preferment did not look kindly on reforms that threatened their privileged positions.

*Stalin had directed the Soviet economy by means of the FYPs. At his death in 1953, the Fifth Plan had run half its course. Its emphasis, as with the preceding ones, had been on heavy industry. When Khrushchev, continuing where Malenkov had left off, sought to re-orientate industry towards consumer production he had to break down the resistance of planners who had grown up on the notion that consumer goods were of only marginal importance. They still measured economic success in terms of iron and steel output. This was a legacy of Stalin's concept of a siege or war economy. It is true that even after Stalin the USSR remained heavily committed to military development in both the nuclear and conventional fields, but it was Khrushchev's genuine belief that if this could be lessened the economic freedom it would give would provide the Soviet Union with the potential to catch up with the West. The USSR's lead in space technology, a by-product of its missile programme, was a remarkable but isolated achievement. It was not matched in any other aspect of its economy.

A Sixth FYP was introduced in 1955, only to be scrapped as being too optimistic and replaced by a Seven-Year Plan in 1959. Under Khrushchev's instructions this Plan had been drawn up with the aim of promoting consumer goods, light industry, chemicals and plastics. In addition, emphasis was placed upon the need for regional development. Less spectacularly than in agriculture, but no less significantly, Khrushchev was endeavouring to reverse a major feature of Stalin's policy. It was a recognition that the USSR could not develop as a modern state unless it brought a much greater degree of balance into its economic structure. An idea of how far Khrushchev's industrial policies succeeded during the period of his leadership can be gained from the performance figures below, comparing the targets in the Seven-Year Plan with the actual performance in 1965:

	Plan	Actual
Gross National Income	162–165	158
(calculated from a unit of 100 in 1958)		
Output		
Industrial goods (unit of 100 in 1958)	185–188	196
Consumer goods (unit of 100 in 1958)	162–165	160
Steel (million tons)	86–91	91
Oil (million tons)	230–240	242
Mineral Fertilisers (million tons)	35	32
Grain (million tons)	164–180	121
Meat (million tons)	6.1	5.25
Workers employed (millions)	66.5	76.9
Total of Available Housing	650–660	72.9
(million square metres)		

Set against the general success of the Seven-Year Plan, the obvious and serious failures were in under-production of grain and meat, and in the inability to deal with the perennial Soviet problem of shortage of accommodation.

6 Co-Existence

The policy of co-existence, as pursued by Khrushchev, was the practical recognition of the right of individual nations to operate the political and social systems of their choice. The acceptance of this right marked a major change of direction in Soviet attitudes to the outside world. The revolutionaries of 1917 had seen themselves as crusaders, intent on fighting the international class war foretold by Marx. The realities of world politics had obliged Lenin and Stalin to suspend the pursuit of this objective, but the commitment to international revolution had never been formally abandoned. Khrushchev, in his secret speech to the Twentieth Party Congress in 1956, took the highly significant step of declaring that a violent conflict between the Communist and capitalist world was not inevitable in the way that Lenin had described. This declaration helped to prepare the way for the moves towards co-existence that are a characteristic of Soviet foreign policy under Khrushchev in the decade after 1956.

The path towards better relations with the West had already been smoothed by a number of developments in the period after Stalin's death. The Korean War, which had soured international relations, ended in 1953. In the following year the USSR joined with the USA and Britain at Geneva in helping to negotiate the withdrawal of French forces from Indo-China. In 1955 the Soviet Union signed a peace treaty with Austria and recalled the army of occupation, stationed there since 1945. The easier atmosphere, referred to as 'the spirit of Geneva', that all this created led the USSR to attend a summit conference in Geneva in the summer of 1955. Khrushchev and Bulganin met President Eisenhower and the French and British Prime Ministers. Although no major agreements were reached, the greater cordiality produced by personal meetings at top level encouraged Khrushchev to believe that the Soviet Union stood to gain by following a policy of co-existence with, rather than hostility towards, the West. Accompanied usually by Bulganin, he began a series of visits to countries outside the Eastern bloc, something that would have been unthinkable in Stalin's time. India, China, Yugoslavia, Britain and the USA were among the countries visited.

On the whole these travels were a propaganda success. He was able to boast of Soviet achievements in space, calling particular attention to the launching of the 'Sputnik' satellite in 1957. He defended the Soviet system with great passion and considerable wit, showing the West that there was a human face to Soviet leadership. He made a remarkable impact in the United States. It was there that he stressed that the development of nuclear weapons in both East and West had rendered obsolete the idea of settling Communist-capitalist differences by recourse to war. Khrushchev's meetings with Eisenhower in 1959 at Camp David were so constructive that they gave rise to the term 'the spirit of Camp David' as an expression of the improved Soviet–American understanding.

*However, it soon became clear how fragile such an understanding was when set against the underlying reality of the Cold War. In 1960 a

Paris summit conference broke up in acrimony when Khrushchev announced that the USSR had shot down an American U2 reconnaissance-plane spying over Soviet territory. Khrushchev made an issue of Eisenhower's refusal to apologise and stormed dramatically out of the conference. A meeting with the new American President, J. F. Kennedy, in Vienna in 1961 proved cordial but it did not repair the earlier damage. Indeed, despite their apparent mutual respect, Khrushchev and Kennedy were shortly to be at loggerheads over arguably the most dangerous East–West confrontation of the Cold War, the Cuban missile crisis of 1962.

The truth was that, although co-existence was attractive as a basic approach to international affairs, it proved hard to sustain in the face of the recurrent crises over such unresolved Cold War issues as Germany and the arms race. Nonetheless, it was in regard to the arms race that Khrushchev gained the greatest success in his policy of co-existence, the signing by the super-powers of a Nuclear-Test Ban Treaty in October 1963. The agreement between the USA and the USSR to abandon nuclear detonations in the atmosphere was the first major accord on arms limitation in the history of the Cold War.

7 Khrushchev and Germany

Khrushchev inherited a chronic crisis in the shape of the German question. It was to preoccupy him for the whole of his leadership. When the European war ended in 1945, the new political shape of the continent had effectively already been decided. In its push westwards the USSR had overrun a large part of eastern Europe, including the eastern third of Germany. Within that area was the capital, Berlin, lying 100 miles inside the Soviet zone. In accordance with the Yalta agreements, Berlin, as with greater Germany, was divided into four occupation zones. Within a short time the three areas of the city occupied by the Western Allies amalgamated as West Berlin, a Western enclave in Communist territory. All future German questions were to have Berlin at their centre. The Yalta agreement stipulated that at some point in the near future the occupying powers would withdraw from Germany and the country would be reunited. However, as the Cold War developed in the late 1940s, a series of disputes between the USSR and the other three occupying powers made the East–West economic and political division of Germany and Berlin an enduring reality. Failing a formal peace treaty between Germany and the former Allies of World War II, the status of the two Germanies would remain a matter of dispute.

With access to Marshall Aid, West Germany and West Berlin began to make a remarkable economic recovery. This contrasted sharply with the poverty of East Germany and East Berlin, mainly caused by a lack of resources and investment. The disparity became a scandal and an embarrassment to the East German authorities and to the Soviet Union. Nor was it simply a matter of economics; the political freedom and open life-style of the West Berliners proved a powerful temptation to East Germans, which no amount of Soviet propaganda could dispel. In the eight years after 1949 over two million refugees fled from East Germany to the West, by way of West Berlin. Many of these were professional and skilled workers whom the DDR (East Germany) could ill afford to lose.

*This was the chief problem that Khrushchev faced. He spoke of his intention to 'block up the drain'. His first moves were to try to force the Western powers to recognise the existence of a separate state of East Germany (the DDR), something which they had consistently refused to do. In 1955 a USSR–DDR treaty was drawn up, granting East Germany full freedom in the conduct of its foreign affairs. However, in explaining the treaty to the United States, Khrushchev announced that the USSR would continue to be the deciding authority in questions relating to rights of movement between West Berlin and West Germany:

1 As for control over the movement between the German Federal Republic (West Germany) and West Berlin of military personnel and freight, of garrisons of the USA, Great Britain and France quartered in West Berlin, in negotiations between the Govern-
5 ments of the USSR and the German Democratic Republic, it was stipulated that this control would henceforth be carried out by the command of the Soviet military forces in Germany temporarily until the achievement of a suitable agreement.
(Note from the Government of the USSR to the Government of
10   the USA, 18 October 1955)

Khrushchev's Note was part-threat, part-offer, to the West. By retaining responsibility for all questions of Western access to Berlin the USSR was delaying the moment when the West would have to deal directly with East Germany. If the West ignored his offer and refused to recognise the legitimacy of the DDR, then the USSR would proceed to hand over to East Germany the management of the access routes. This would enforce on the West the *de facto* recognition of the DDR, since there would be no alternative to direct relations with it once the USSR withdrew. This would destroy the fiction with which the West still persisted, that East Germany was merely the Soviet zone of occupied Germany.

*In the event, the USA called his bluff by refusing to change its diplomatic position on Germany. Khrushchev took no action. By 1958 the DDR had still not gained formal Western recognition as a sovereign state. To press the issue, in October of that year Khrushchev informed the West that the Soviet Union intended to hand over to the DDR full control of its own affairs. He then delivered an ultimatum. In strong language he accused the West of using West Berlin 'as a springboard for espionage and anti-Soviet acts'. He warned that if within six months the West had not responded positively, the USSR would sign a separate peace treaty with the DDR. This would directly threaten the independence of West Berlin since, as a sovereign state, the DDR would have the right to claim the whole of its capital, Berlin:

1 Berlin is a smouldering fuse that has been connected to a powder keg. Incidents arising here may, in an atmosphere of heated passions, suspicions and mutual apprehensions, cause a conflagration which will be difficult to extinguish.

5   The Soviet Government proposes to make no change in the present procedure for military traffic of the USA, Great Britain and France from West Berlin to the Federal Republic of Germany for half a year. If the above period is not utilised to reach an adequate agreement, the Soviet Union will then carry out the
10 planned measures through an agreement with the DDR.

> (Note from the Government of the USSR to
> the Governments of France, Great Britain and
> the USA, 27 November 1958)

Khrushchev's ultimatum created an international crisis, but it is unlikely that he was doing more than checking how committed the West was to the defence of Berlin. The Western powers pointedly delayed their formal reply to Khrushchev's Note, but let it be known that they regarded the six-month ultimatum as outrageous. When the USA, on behalf of the West, did reply it was in the form of an unequivocal reassertion of the right of continued free access to West Berlin. Faced with this, Khrushchev withdrew the ultimatum and at a summit meeting in March 1959 admitted the rights of the three occupying powers in West Berlin. In a series of summit meetings with the American Presidents, Eisenhower and Kennedy, Khrushchev modified his demands but continued to insist that the Berlin question, 'that fishbone in the gullet' as he called it, must be resolved.

*Having temporarily tried the gentler approach, Khrushchev then returned to the attack. In June 1961 he met Kennedy again. This time he repeated his warning that the Western powers must be prepared to leave Berlin within six months. The effect of this threat was to increase the flight of refugees from East to West Berlin; 1000 a day became the average figure in the summer of 1961. Unable to staunch the haemorrhage by other means, the East German leader, Walter Ulbricht, ordered the construction of the Berlin Wall, the physical symbol of the ideological East–West divide. Initial fears were that the Wall, which split the city in half, would lead to open conflict. However, in an odd way it created greater international understanding. It clarified the diplomatic differences that had led to its construction and, by stopping the loss of essential manpower, it saved East Germany from economic collapse. This helped to restore stability and consequently lessened the likelihood of desperate measures being taken by the East Germans, which the Soviet Union would then have had to support and the West would have had to resist.

The inconsistency of Khrushchev's approach to the West over Germany is explained as much by the pressures upon him in the Soviet Union as by the intrinsic merits of the German question. Khrushchev was conscious that his style of leadership needed positive successes in order to justify itself. He was constantly under scrutiny. Had he been able to settle the German and Berlin issues in a manner that brought benefit and credit to the Eastern bloc and the Soviet Union this would have been an outstanding achievement, and would have considerably enhanced his position in the USSR. In the main, however, he was thwarted by the strength of the commitment of the United States to defend West Germany. In addition, the persistent and glaring economic weakness of East Germany undermined Khrushchev's diplomatic bargaining position. He was never able to realise his main aim of obtaining Western acceptance of separate German peace treaties. Behind Khrushchev's ultimata and blustering was his sure knowledge that a genuine settlement of the German problem could not be gained by unilateral Soviet action. It would require a formal and binding agreement between the USA and the USSR.

Although the Berlin Wall helped stabilise the situation in 1961, its construction marked the failure of Khrushchev's German policy up to that point. He and the USSR had suffered a serious international reverse. His subsequent behaviour in 1962 in regard to Cuba may well represent an attempt to recover the prestige lost over Germany.

*Khrushchev's last initiative on the German front was an attempt to win by persuasion what he had been unable to achieve by threat. He made direct contact with the West German government, sent his son-in-law to Bonn to organise a series of official visits and let it be known that he was prepared to try to solve the Berlin issue by by-passing the East Germans in order to deal directly with Bonn. This was a drastic reversal of all previous Soviet policy and not unnaturally provoked a bitter response from Ulbricht and the East Germans. The change also puzzled many in the Soviet Union. Khrushchev had apparently become convinced that there was no future in enforcing a German settlement on the West. That had been tried and it had failed. Approaching the West German government directly was a striking piece of diplomacy that might well give the USSR an advantage in future negotiations. There were also rumours that, at a personal level, Khrushchev found Ulbricht and the East German government a wearisome bunch, whom he preferred to ignore if he could. Whatever Khrushchev's motives, they soon became academic, since, before anything could come of his new German policy, he had been removed from office in the Soviet Union.

8 The Cuban Missile Crisis

When Fidel Castro, the revolutionary leader of Cuba since 1959, openly declared himself a Communist and began to take steps to end the USA's economic domination of the island, Khrushchev saw the possibility of a major Cold-War coup for the USSR. He moved in quickly, arranging for the Soviet Union to buy up Cuba's sugar crop and offering other economic assistance. The attraction of Cuba for the Soviet Union was obvious. It was an opportunity for the USSR to establish a firm foothold in the western hemisphere. The Soviet Union hoped, and the USA feared, that the creation of a Russian-backed Marxist state in Cuba would mark the prelude to the rapid spread of Soviet-style Communism throughout central and Latin America.

*Aware of United States' bitterness, Khrushchev warned that the USSR would be prepared to act if the USA used force against Cuba. The Soviet Union increased its investment and involvement in Cuba, culminating in the installation on the island of Soviet nuclear missiles, capable of reaching almost every state in the USA. Khrushchev's stated justification for Soviet actions was that the nuclear devices were there to defend Cuba against possible American intervention. But, since this claim followed a previous denial that the USSR had installed any missiles at all, the argument was unconvincing. Kennedy announced a naval blockade of Cuba until the missiles were removed, and let it be known that if any attempt were made to use them against the USA he would order a retaliation in kind. When Khrushchev likened the proximity of Russian weapons in Cuba to that of American missiles in Turkey, the USSR's neighbour, Kennedy replied that the American rocket-bases were there to defend Europe, whereas the only conceivable purpose of the Soviet missiles in Cuba was to threaten the USA with direct nuclear attack. Kennedy backed his ultimatum by placing the US armed forces on nuclear war alert.

Faced by such uncompromising determination, Khrushchev chose not to risk a full-scale nuclear confrontation. He gave the order for the Soviet ships which were approaching the exclusion zone to put about and not to challenge the American naval blockade. With the tension broken, direct contacts by letter and phone were made between Kennedy and Khrushchev. The result of their exchanges was the Soviet leader's promise to order the withdrawal of Soviet missiles from Cuba and the American President's commitment to reduce the USA's bases in Turkey. This latter agreement was no small gain for the USSR, but at the time it was overshadowed by what appeared to observers in the Soviet Union as a major diplomatic victory for the Americans. It had been the USSR which had backed off. The USA had reasserted its paramount influence in the western hemisphere. This apparent defeat damaged the USSR's international standing and led to serious criticism of Khrushchev within the Soviet Union.

9 Khrushchev and China

The coming to power in China of the Communists under Mao Tse-tung in 1949 had been welcomed in Moscow. It was logical for the Soviet Union to think that it now had a major Marxist ally in its Cold-War struggle with the West. Indeed, that is precisely what the West feared, the formation of a huge Soviet-dominated, Communist power-bloc that stretched eastwards from Europe to the Pacific. But appearances were deceptive. There was no real harmony between Moscow and Peking. Relations between the USSR and Communist China had never been easy [See page 74]. Stalin's Russia, pre-occupied with its own internal problems, had failed to grasp the significance of developments in Mao Tse-tung's China.

The fundamental issue in relations between Red China and the Soviet Union was the competition to decide which of them was the real leader of the Communist world. Was it the USSR, product and guardian of the great 1917 revolution, or the People's Republic of China with its fresh revolutionary ideas and massive population? According to traditional Marxist analysis, true proletarian revolution could occur only in an urban, industrial society. In the judgement of Soviet theorists China, which was a rural and agricultural society, could not be regarded as a fully developed Communist state. Soviet references to the inferiority of the Chinese model aroused the anger of Maoists, who retaliated by accusing the USSR of betraying the cause of world revolution. This referred to Khrushchev's attempts in the 1950s to move towards a policy of co-existence with the West. It was ironic that, although the death of Stalin in 1953 had removed an obvious personal obstacle to better Sino-Soviet relations, Khrushchev's subsequent treatment of the Stalin legend re-awakened Chinese suspicions. His extraordinary assault on Stalin's 'cult of personality' was interpreted in China as a scarcely veiled attack on Mao's own brand of highly-personalised leadership.

*Despite occasional appearances of understanding, Sino-Soviet animosity increased throughout the 1950s. Mao acknowledged the special position of the Soviet Union in the history of proletarian struggle, but he also let it be known that he regarded Khrushchev's current attitude towards the West as too soft. Mao demanded that the USSR show greater commitment to liberation movements worldwide and abandon 'revisionism', the word for heresy in Marxist vocabulary. In 1957 the Chinese were offered Soviet assistance in developing their own nuclear weapon, but in return Moscow wanted control of Peking's defence policy. The price was too high. Mao rejected the offer, opting instead for a slower but independent Chinese nuclear programme. China was not prepared to play a subordinate role to the USSR.

This became abundantly clear in the following year when Sino-American relations reached breaking point over the United States' military support for Nationalist China in Taiwan. In the ensuing crisis Mao expected the USSR to provide Communist China with diplomatic, if not military, backing. However, the Soviet Union had no wish to become involved. Khrushchev declared 'the time is not ripe for the socialist world to test the stability of the capitalist system' and refused to make any commitment to the Chinese Communists. To Mao, this was further proof of Khrushchev's betrayal of the international Communist cause.

*These profound disagreements over foreign policy and Marxist ideology were deepened by disputes over territory. In the late 1950s and 1960s both countries stationed large numbers of troops along their joint border in central Asia. Incidents were frequent and threatened to lead to a major confrontation. When a border war between China and India broke out in 1962 the USSR remained officially neutral, but unofficially let it be known that it supported the Indian case, thereby widening the Sino-Soviet gap still further. In the same year that gap became a gulf as a result of the Cuban missile crisis. China fiercely criticised the Soviet Union on two counts: first, for siting its rockets in such a detectable manner and location; second, for its craven submission to the American ultimatum.

1963 marked the lowest point in the relations of the two Communist powers. China refused to join the USA and the USSR in signing the Test-Ban Treaty. Moscow condemned this as certain proof of Mao's and China's irresponsibility. Khrushchev claimed that China wanted to see the old world, capitalist and Communist, engage in mutual nuclear destruction, thus leaving her free to dominate the world that remained. Mao responded by denouncing the Soviet Union for reneging on its revolutionary duty: 'Soviet revisionist collaborators are uniting with the running dogs of capitalism'. The Soviet Union reverted to Russian tradition by talking of the 'yellow peril', the spectre of the vast population of China overrunning Europe from the east, with Russia as the first victim. At an ideological level, Mao and his colleagues were branded as 'petty bourgeois', not true proletarian revolutionaries. Mao's retaliation was to dismiss the Soviet leaders as 'fascists, unworthy of the Marxist–Leninist inheritance'. These were not merely insults; by characterising Khrushchev and the Kremlin as the betrayers of revolution, Mao was encouraging Communists in all other countries to reject the Soviet lead and turn to the Chinese model of Marxism.

There was a markedly personal element in all this. Khrushchev and Mao Tse-tung appear to have conceived a deep distaste for each other. Khrushchev referred to Mao as 'a living corpse', while Mao spoke of the Soviet leader as 'an old boot that you throw into the corner because it is no longer of any use'. Western observers often found such exchanges quaint and comic, but behind the insults there was a deadly serious battle taking place for ascendancy in the Communist world. Instead of developing into the great monolith that the West had feared, international Communism had become a divided force. China and the Soviet Union, the two Marxist giants, were engaged in a bitter competition to win or to retain the loyalty and support of the rest of the Communist world. The public squabbling brought Khrushchev little credit and the scandal of Sino-Soviet disharmony was a factor in the weakening of his position within the USSR. At the time of his fall from power in 1964, which by coincidence was the same month in which China exploded its first atomic bomb, Khrushchev was still trying to rally the Communist world against the Chinese heretics.

10 The Fall of Khrushchev

In October 1964 Khrushchev took a holiday at a Black Sea resort. During his absence from Moscow the Politburo met and decided on his removal as leader. A meeting of the Central Committee was convened and Khrushchev was summoned back to Moscow to appear before it. When he attended he was informed that he had retired through age and poor-health and that the positions he had held had been filled by Leonid Brezhnev and Alexei Kosygin. The news was publicly announced on the radio and in *Pravda*. The other Moscow newspaper, *Izvestia*, whose editor was Khrushchev's son-in-law, was not permitted to publish that day. Accepting that he had been wholly outmanoeuvred, that he had no allies and that it was useless to resist, Khrushchev slipped away into obscure retirement. Some days later *Pravda* published a lengthy editorial in which, without referring to him by name, Khrushchev's weaknesses and errors were listed:

1   The Leninist Party is the enemy of subjectivism, individualism and drifting in Communist construction, of hare-brained scheme-making, of half-baked conclusions and hasty decisions and actions taken without regard to realities. Bragging and phrase-
5   mongering, bossiness, reluctance to take account of scientific achievement and practical experience are alien to it.

   It is only on the Leninist principle of collective leadership that it is possible to direct and develop the increasing creative initiative of the Party.

*The manner of Khrushchev's demotion and the substance of *Pravda*'s criticisms are instructive. Whatever his achievements may have been in the previous decade, it is clear that by the autumn of 1964 he was politically friendless and isolated. However necessary de-Stalinisation may have been, Khrushchev, by introducing it, had provided the grounds for his own eventual dismissal. The attack upon 'the cult of personality' created the language and the justification for removing any subsequent leader whose personal authority grew too large. In Stalin's time his subordinates were too frightened to oppose him. This had never been so with Khrushchev. He had had to overcome challenges in the 1950s, and the reason that there was no organised move against him until 1964 is to be explained by a lack of opportunity rather than by a lack of will. All Stalin's colleagues had owed their positions directly to his patronage. Khrushchev never wielded that same authority. It is true that some of the middle and lower rank officials were his proteges, but he never had the control of the Party and governmental machine that Stalin had possessed. The members of the collective leadership that succeeded Stalin owed nothing to Khrushchev for the positions they held. Even in his best years as leader, Khrushchev was ultimately answerable to the Politburo and Central Committee whose members were individually his political equals and collectively his master. Of course, in any political system strength of personality counts for a good deal. In the earlier years of his leadership, Khrushchev's gregarious style and jocular approach made a refreshing and welcome change from the grim joylessness of Stalinism. But these attributes were of advantage only when things were going well for him. As the *Pravda* editorial made clear, when his reputation began to wane his style and manner were characterised as personal failings.

*Khrushchev was a highly industrious leader of the Soviet Union, and made himself very visible. He took a direct part in a wide range of domestic and foreign affairs. This close personal involvement had its obvious advantages, but it also made him vulnerable. When policies failed, he appeared directly responsible in a way that a less energetic leader would not have been. There was no single event that caused his fall into disfavour. It is rather that as time went by his policy failures tended to outweigh his successes. Dissatisfaction accumulated. With hindsight, it is possible to identify those areas of growing opposition and to determine why, by 1964, Khrushchev had no signficiant political support on which he could rely.

Khrushchev's attempts to streamline and decentralise many areas of Party and government involved him in a continuous struggle with the forces of Soviet bureaucracy. Stalinism had been a heavily bureaucratic system. The Communist Party under Stalin had been the great dispenser of jobs and patronage. When Khrushchev sought to rational-ise the system and make it more effective he challenged the privileges, if not the livelihood, of a whole army of officials and functionaries. They were hardly likely to regret his political relegation.

*A more dramatic and far-reaching rejection of the old ways had been Khrushchev's de-Stalinisation initiative. This had been a calculated risk. He was aware of how ingrained Stalinism was in the USSR. After decades of Stalin-worship, it was a huge psychological wrench for Party members to admit that the great leader had been so wrong in so many ways. Some of the old guard, such as Molotov and Kaganovich, could not bring themselves to accept the total destruction of the Stalin legend. For the sake of expediency, they went along with de-Stalinisation, but they remained fearful of what it might incidentally reveal about their own past. They thought also that it threatened the claims and reputation of the Party. Moreover, the greater freedom of expression given to writers and artists in the post-Stalin 'thaw' seemed to them to be an added and unnecessary danger. The Party die-hards did not easily forgive Khrushchev for placing such hazards in the path of traditional Soviet Communism.

*In his rise to prominence in the mid-1950s Khrushchev had been able to rely on the considerable backing of the leaders of the armed forces, but by 1964 that support had been largely forfeited. This was mainly the result of his wish to cut or redirect military expenditure. By the mid-1950s the USSR could genuinely be defined as a super-power; the country matched the USA in its possession of the H-bomb and was beginning to make significant advances in missile development. Khrushchev felt that this justified a cut-back in conventional forces. In 1960 he proposed reducing the armed services by over a million men, a cut of one third. Such developments, taken together with the loss of Soviet military prestige over Cuba, meant that by 1964 he had exhausted the goodwill of the generals.

*In foreign affars, to which he had devoted so much of his energy, Khrushchev suffered a similar decline in his fortunes. In personal terms there was no doubt that he had become a truly international statesman; his breadth of vision and direct experience of summit diplomacy was unprecedented in Soviet tradition. Despite this, there were few successes to which he could point. He had entered into a long, embarrassing and unresolved conflict with China to retain the moral leadership of the USSR in the Communist world. He had awakened hopes of independence in the Eastern-bloc countries, only to dash them by military intervention and the reimposition of the sternest Soviet control. He had fought a running Cold War battle with the West over Germany, but had been unable to deliver the peace treaty by which he had set such store. He had then dismayed the East Germans by his overtures to Bonn. Almost as a last throw he had tried to recover his diplomatic losses by the installation of Soviet missiles in Cuba, only to have to back down in the face of American determination. These undeniable failures aroused bitterness in his Kremlin colleagues.

*The severest measure by which leaders are judged, whether in capitalist or Communist countries, is the economic one. Khrushchev had promised a more productive Soviet economy, geared to the interests of the consumer but still capable of overhauling the West. It was a brave but unrealistic boast. Advances were made, but the basic problems inherited from Stalin were still there in the mid-1960s. Ironically, his most far-sighted policy, the reclamation of the virgin lands, was the one which, in his own time, brought him the greatest criticism. Its apparent misjudgement as a policy did more than any other single failure to discredit him.

Those involved in the plot to oust him in 1964 could be confident that the range of Soviet interests angered or disillusioned by Khrushchev's policies during the previous eight years was such that there would be little resistance to his removal.

Making notes on 'Khrushchev'

Your notes on this chapter should provide you with an outline of Khrushchev's career before 1953, but your major task is to provide yourself with material concerning the changes brought about in the Soviet Union during Khrushchev's period of leadership. This should cover both domestic and foreign affairs. The following headings, sub-headings and questions should help you.

1   **Early Career**
1.1   Trace the main biographical outline.
2   **His Rise**
2.1   The political situation in the Soviet Union after Stalin's death. How had Khrushchev manoeuvred himself into a position of authority by 1956?
3   **De-Stalinisation**
3.1   The 'secret speech'.
3.2   What were Khrushchev's motives in denouncing Stalin?
4   **De-Stalinisation and the Soviet Satellites**
4.1   How did the satellites interpret the 'secret speech'?
4.2   The Hungarian rising in 1956.
5   **Khrushchev and the Soviet economy**
5.1   What were the main features of the virgin-lands policy? How far did it succeed?
5.2.1 The essentials of Khrushchev's industrial strategy.
5.2.2 Compare the aims and results of the Seven Year Plan.
6   **Co-existence**
6.1   Why was this such a significant departure in Soviet foreign policy?
7   **Khrushchev and Germany**
7.1   Describe the German problem that Khrushchev inherited.
7.2   How close did he come to solving the problem?
8   **The Cuban-Missile Crisis**
8.1   What did Khrushchev hope to gain by the installation of the missiles?

8.2   How serious a diplomatic defeat for Khrushchev was the outcome of the crisis?

9   Khrushchev and China

9.1   The basic issues dividing China and the USSR.

9.2   How far was Khrushchev personally responsible for Sino-Soviet rivalry?

10   Khrushchev's Fall

10.1   The immediate circumstances of his dismissal.

10.2   The nature of Khrushchev's power compared to Stalin's.

10.3   Identify the main areas of opposition to Khrushchev that had arisen by 1964.

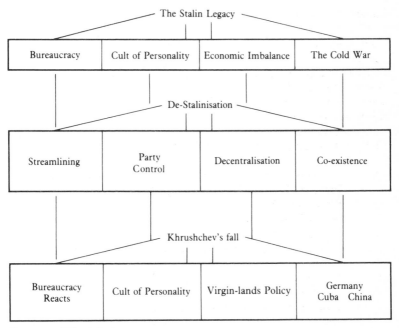

Summary – 'Khrushchev'

Answering essay questions on 'Khrushchev'

The questions set by examiners on this topic are invariably drawn from three key areas: the reasons for Khrushchev's rise, his policy of de-Stalinisation, and the reasons for his fall. If you take a comparative approach, contrasting Khrushchev's policies with those of Stalin, you will provide yourself with an effective basis from which to answer questions on all three areas. You may be asked a direct question such as 'Describe and analyse the major changes introduced by Khrushchev into the USSR in the period 1956–64'. This is a sound basic question to prepare, as it touches on all the major themes of the period 1953–64. Make a list of the characteristics of de-Stalinisation and its effects. It may be helpful to group these into sets and sub-sets, eg. a) domestic policy – the reform of the economy, the attack upon bureaucracy, 'the thaw'; b) foreign policy – co-existence, the Soviet satellites, the German question, Sino-Soviet rivalry. These sets may then be used as a frame of reference to which any question on the post-Stalin period can be related. While you may be asked a broad question, such as the one given above, it is more likely that you will be asked variations on this central theme. Here are some examples:

1 Why were the other members of the post-1953 collective leadership unable to prevent Khrushchev from assuming power in the mid-1950s?
2 Examine the importance of the Twentieth Congress of the CPSU (1956).
3 How successful was Khrushchev's policy of de-Stalinisation?
4 Consider the view that Khrushchev fell from power in 1964 because 'he had tried to do too much, too soon'.

Prepare an essay plan for question 2. In order to tackle the question of 'importance' you have first to describe what took place at the Congress. Your opening paragraph should set the pattern for the answer by doing this. It should refer to the key points in Khrushchev's Secret Report. This speech is clearly the centre-piece of your answer and should form the main part of the essay. Stress the importance of the speech as the public starting-point of de-Stalinisation, pointing out that all subsequent adjustments in regard to internal and foreign policies under Khrushchev took their justification from the dramatic revelations in his Congress report.

Questions, such as 4 above, on why Khrushchev fell are popular with examiners for the very good reason that they provide an excellent way of testing candidates' understanding of the period overall. You are strongly encouraged, therefore, to prepare an essay plan for question 4. Obviously, you need to address yourself directly to the quotation by describing what Khrushchev attempted to do. Draw on your two lists to indicate his domestic and foreign policy initiatives. When you have established this in your opening paragraphs you will be in a position to begin judging the 'too much, too soon' aspects. The question of the volume and the speed of his attempted reforms points you to the nature of the problems confronting Khrushchev in the post-Stalin era. The Stalin legacy, the inertia of the bureaucracy and the resistance of Soviet vested interests to change meant that Khrushchev faced great obstacles. Ask yourself whether he tackled these in the most effective way. Were there genuine alternatives? Did he have the necessary time? Try to link your points together, so that they provide a coherent response to the question and justify the conclusion that you offer in your final paragraph.

Source-based questions on 'Khrushchev'

1 De-Stalinisation
Read the extracts from Khrushchev's 1949 speech on page 95, and from the 'secret speech' on pages 99 and 102 and answer the following questions:
a) According to his statement in 1949, how highly did Khrushchev rate Stalin in Communist tradition?
b) As revealed in the 'secret speech', what fate befell the Central Committee elected by the Seventeenth Party Congress?
c) What features of the purges are portrayed by Khrushchev's description of the treatment of 'Comrade Eikhe' (page 99, lines 30–35)?
d) How does the account of Stalin's relations with Tito (page 102) illustrate the concept of 'the cult of personality'?
e) Explain the marked difference in tone between Khrushchev's 1949 and 1956 speeches.

2 The Seven Year Plan
Study the table on page 106 and then answer the following questions:
a) According to the statistics, which areas of the economy came closest to reaching the Plan's targets?
b) Why is there such an emphasis in the Plan on consumer goods?
c) How would you account for the gap between the target figures for accommodation and the actual figures?
d) What do these statistics contribute to an understanding of the aims and results of Khrushchev's agricultural policies?

3 The German Question
Read the extracts from the official Notes on pages 109 and 110, and then answer the following questions:
a) What diplomatic threat is implied in the Note of October 1955?
b) Explain what the USSR means by its statement in the 1958 Note (line 1) that 'Berlin is a smouldering fuse that has been connected to a powder keg'.
c) What are the 'planned measures' referred to in line 10 of this Note?
d) In what ways do these two Notes illustrate Khrushchev's approach to the German question?

CHAPTER 7

The Soviet Record, 1924–64

In Chapter 1 it was suggested that the problems of the period could be expressed in three questions relating to the political power structure, the economy and foreign relations. Let us assess the record of Stalin and Khrushchev by offering answers to those same questions.

1 The Exercise of Power

How would power be exercised in the Soviet state, and by whom?

It is one of the many paradoxes of Soviet history that the Communist movement, which in theory drew its authority from the will of the masses, should have become so dependent on the idea of the great leader. It was the memory of Lenin's dominance of the Bolshevik Party that endured as the most powerful legacy of the 1917 Revolution. Lenin's practical skills had been necessary to put Marx's ideas into effect. After 1917 reverence for the achievements of Lenin as Party leader became a vital part of Communist tradition. It was Stalin's ability to suggest that he was continuing the work of Lenin that eased his own path to supremacy in the USSR after 1924. Circumstances had made loyalty to the Party and loyalty to Lenin inseparable. Similarly, by the late 1920s Stalin had succeeded in identifying his own authority with that of the rule of the Party. This made it extremely difficult for his fellow Communists to oppose him. To criticise Stalin was equivalent to doubting Lenin, the Party and the Revolution.

Stalin's intimate knowledge of the workings of the Secretariat aided him in his rise to power. By 1924 he had come to hold a number of important administrative positions, chief of which was the office of General Secretary of the CPSU. This left him ideally placed to monitor and control the appointment of members to the various posts within the Party's gift. Stalin soon became the indispensable link-man in the growing Soviet system of government. Large numbers of Communist officials owed their positions to Stalin's influence. They could not afford to be disloyal to him. This gave him a power-base which his Party rivals could not match. In the 1920s he was able to defeat all other contenders in the power struggle that followed Lenin's death. The clear proof of how powerful Stalin had become was evident in the 1930s when he launched a series of purges of his real or imagined enemies in the government, the armed services and the Party. From then until his death in 1953, he exercised absolute authority over the Soviet Union.

Consider the following views:

1 Stalinism was more than Stalinism: it was Leninism too. Instead

of thinking of Stalin as Lenin's Judas, we should think of him as
Lenin's admired protege. The two got on together very well and
nothing has been more misleading, more calculated to give a
5 totally wrong idea of the Soviet system, and Lenin himself, than
the way the two have been forced apart by Lenin's idolators and
Stalin's enemies. Trotsky, of course, had good reason for presenting Stalin as an inferior. But this does not excuse all those ardent
apologists for Lenin's revolution who would rather ignore the
10 millions consigned to Gulag (started by Lenin, not Stalin –
though not under that name) than admit that their most cherished
beliefs had no foundation.

(Edward Crankshaw)

15 There are numerous differences between Leninism and Stalinism. Leninism meant first and foremost the rule of the Party,
albeit of its self-elected elite . . . Stalinism was founded on two
pillars, the Party and the government, and both were under the
supervision of the political police. Stalin maintained many
20 sources of information, since reliance on one source would have
been dangerous. One rationale for the purges was that they
removed many of the existing information providers and replaced
them with new men and women who were duty bound to criticise
the views of their predecessors. Under Lenin there was nothing
25 like this concentration of power.

(Martin McCauley)

*A continuing argument among scholars is whether the totalitarian-
ism of Stalin was a logical progression from the authoritarianism of
Lenin, or whether it was the responsibility of Stalin alone. Isaac
Deutscher and Roy Medvedev, both of whom suffered under Stalin,
follow Trotsky in believing that Stalin perverted the basically democratic nature of Leninism into a personal dictatorship. In contrast, Edward
Crankshaw and Robert Conquest regard Stalin's tyranny as simply the
fully developed form of Lenin's essentially repressive creed of revolution. Alexander Solzhenitsyn, a leading Soviet writer who survived long
imprisonment in one of Stalin's labour camps, regards Stalin as a
'blind, mechanical executor of Lenin's will' and points to the fact that
all the apparatus of Stalin's authority was in place before he took over.
The one-party state, the secret police, the attack upon factionalism
within the Party; all this existed in 1924.

Despite the enormous personal power that Stalin wielded, his
constant assertion was that he held that power by the will of the Party.
In practice, his personal authority from the 1930s onwards, secured by
ruthless purging, put him above the Party. He became answerable to
no-one. Khrushchev, his successor as Party and government leader
between 1956 and 1964, was never in a comparable position. Although

he became both General Secretary and Premier, his personal power was not of the same proportions as Stalin's. As a result, when he appeared to go too far in his adjustment of Stalin's policies, Khrushchev's Party colleagues were strong enough to force his removal.

It is tempting to see the Khrushchev years, coming as they did after the grim and deadly tyranny of Stalin, as a period of liberalism. This would be a mistake. It is true that the outgoing and jocular Khrushchev presented a sharp personal contrast to the paranoid Stalin who rarely left the Kremlin. However, despite his apparent playfulness and levity, Khrushchev was a resolute upholder of Communist rule in the USSR and its satellites. He was not a libertarian in any Western sense. He wanted to rid the Soviet system of its many bureaucratic encumbrances but he did not want an open society. The USSR remained in all essentials totalitarian. It was a one-party state dominated by the CPSU. Indeed, it was this that denied Khrushchev absolute power. It is not an exaggeration to say that in his time Stalin had become the Communist Party. Khrushchev never obtained this degree of identification. In the last analysis his authority was always dependent on the support of the Party. When this was withdrawn from him in 1964 Khrushchev had no other political resources on which to draw.

*In his plans for modernising the Soviet Union, Khrushchev made the momentous decision to destroy Stalin's reputation and abandon his policies. In doing this he was seeking to reverse 30 years of Soviet history. This was an enormous task and in the end it proved too much for him. Khrushchev fell from power in 1964 with his objectives largely unfulfilled. The Soviet economy was still under-productive, Soviet standards of living still lagged a long way behind the West and the USSR was still burdened with a huge defence budget. The irony was that for Khrushchev to have undone the work of Stalin he would need to have been another Stalin, but he was never able to exercise that degree of power. Throughout his eight years as Soviet leader, Khrushchev had a constant struggle to maintain his authority over Party and government. His removal from office by the united opposition of his Party colleagues was clear proof that he had not been able to control the political machine as Stalin had done.

One of Stalin's enduring legacies was the resistance of those entrenched in the system created by him to the idea of major change in the Soviet Union. It was not so much that Khrushchev's policies were in themselves defective, as that he tried to do too much, too soon. He faced formidable opposition from those who, having escaped being purged, came to benefit from Stalinism. The Party, the bureaucracy and the Army were the chief beneficiaries and, therefore, the guardians of the system Stalin had bequeathed. In attempting to redirect the Soviet Union, Khrushchev was challenging a whole range of vested interests. It was these interests, the forces of Soviet conservatism, that finally defeated him.

2 The Economy

How would the economy develop under Soviet Communism?

However Stalin's economic policies are measured, historians are in broad agreement that the USSR's industrial revolution between 1928 and 1941 marks a prodigious achievement. The debate is not about the magnitude of the feat, but about the underlying logic and the means used to reach it. Two essential questions dictate the form of the historical controversy: was the industrial programme which Stalin adopted based upon a realistic understanding of the needs of modern Russia and could the USSR have been industrialised except by the brutal methods that Stalin used? With hindsight it can be argued that Stalin's economic strategy was mistaken because it was founded on a distorted view of the West's industrial history. It could be said that Stalin misinterpreted the economic difficulties experienced by the Western economies between the two World Wars. It was true that the West underwent a period of relative decline but that was largely in the old-fashioned staple industries of iron, steel and the associated areas of heavy-goods production, the very areas which Stalin chose for investment and development in the Soviet Union. The Western world recovered by an expansion of light engineering and modern technology, made directly responsive to deliberately-stimulated consumer demand. Stalin purposely turned his back on consumer goods. Under him Soviet growth was to be in the spectacular areas of steel-mills, oil-refineries, hydro-electric plants, tractor factories and the like. These were the symbols of State power. No concessions were to be made in the USSR to the decadent demands of capitalist-inspired consumerism. In a collectivist State the economy had to serve collective needs, not those of the individual. Such an economic standpoint might well have been justifiable in terms of Communist theory, and it clearly expressed Stalin's perception of the immediate requirements of a Soviet State besieged in a hostile Europe, but time was to show that Soviet industrialisation, as envisaged and established by Stalin, would not answer the USSR's long-term needs.

Impressive though it was in its short-term achievements, Stalin's economic revolution committed the Soviet Union to a form of development that made it impossible for it to realise the main objective of catching up with the world's advanced nations. At the very time when the West, through the bitter experience of the Depression, began to realise the need to abandon its reliance on the traditional heavy industries, Stalin's Russia began to adopt them as the basis for her own economic development. The problems that this resulted in (a permanently unbalanced economy, with over-production of non-essentials and under-production of vital commodities, set against the background of a chronic food-shortage) were to outlive Stalin and to confront Khrushchev and his successors.

*Stalin's methods, the enforcement of collectivisation and industrialisation, are equally controversial. Some observers, then and since, have argued that the special history and character of Russia required a Stalin to effect the necessary transformation of society. Their assertion is that without an individual of Stalin's authority to lead the way the Russian people could not have been mobilised on the scale demanded by modernisation. Individual leadership, runs the argument, has been the most consistent and powerful political tradition in Russian history. 1917 did not change this. The autocracy of the Tsars was simply replaced by the autocracy of Lenin, and then of Stalin. Much of Stalin's genuine popularity came from the Russian perception of him as the leader strong enough to put those ever-troublesome peasants in their place and resolute enough to guide the nation to modernity through the birth pangs of industrialisation. Pursuing this line of reasoning, it is even possible to justify the great hardships which befell the Soviet people. Historical comparisons can be used to show that no society has undergone industrialisation without witnessing a significant measure of disturbance and distress. If the Russian experience appears more painful than most, the explanation lies in the speed and intensity of the Soviet model. The climax to this line of argument comes with the suggestion that the sufferings of the Russian people under Stalin's planned economy become historically acceptable when it is remembered that without the enforced industrialisation of the 1930s the Soviet Union could not have sustained itself during the four years of total war from 1941 to 1945. E. H. Carr, while not condoning the means used to achieve it, suggests that without Stalin's 'planned economy' the USSR would have collapsed in war.

*Those historians who are unmoved by this defence of Stalin's methods have responded by pointing out that, in spite of Stalin's claims to be building a war economy, when war did come the USSR was not in fact ready and that it was luck as much as planning that saved the day for Stalin. In addition, it is argued that, for all its apparent achievement of industrial goals under Stalin, the Russian economy could not have expanded at the rate that it did had not a sound basis for growth already existed. Writers such as Leonard Schapiro, have speculated that the style and pace of industrialisation developed by 1914 under Tsarism would, if continued, have reached no less a level of expansion by 1941 than had Stalin's terror strategy. Norman Stone has supported this contention by stressing that it was only because the expertise and basic industrial structures already existed that the Five Year Plans reached the level of success that they did. Robert Conquest, an especially sharp critic of Stalin's totalitarianism, has remarked: 'Stalinism is one way of attaining industrialisation, just as cannibalism is one way of attaining a high protein diet'. Perhaps the most telling censure among Western scholars of Stalin's methods comes from an economic historian. While prepared to give credit to Stalin for the scope of his achievement on the industrial front, Alec Nove reflects:

1   The attempt to go much too fast went altogether too far. The sacrifices imposed were on a scale unparalleled in history in time of peace. The resultant bitterness, disloyalty, repression, also involved a heavy cost, including a military cost. Many Russians
5   greeted the Germans as deliverers from tyranny.

*Those who assert that Stalin's economic policies were mistaken point out that, regardless of the achievement in heavy goods production, the living standards of Soviet factory-workers in 1953 were barely higher than in 1928, while those of farm-workers were actually lower than in 1913. Khrushchev attempted to redress the imbalance. He opted for decentralised planning, industrial diversification and the encouragement of progressive techniques in agriculture. Unfortunately for him, his measures were soundly conceived but poorly applied. In the relatively short period during which he was leader Khrushchev was unable to change the basic character of the Soviet economy.

At the time, Khrushchev received a bad press at home and abroad for the seeming failure of his agricultural policies. This was largely undeserved. He was struggling to put right in a few years the neglect of a quarter of a century. Stalin's subordination of agriculture to the needs of industrialisation had deprived the land of investment and resources. His forced collectivisation programme had disrupted rural life to an extent from which it would take generations to recover. Khrushchev's reforms were basically sound but he was facing an enormous task that in the short-term proved to be beyond the resources at his disposal. The re-introduction of incentives and the attempt to bring waste-land into production were policies that needed time to develop before they could begin to show returns. It was a problem that had beset agricultural reformers in Tsarist as well as revolutionary Russia. Time was the one thing they were never allowed. J. N. Westwood puts in memorably when he observes: 'The virgin lands, on which Khrushchev had staked his reputation, turned out to be an achievement concealed within a failure'.

3 Foreign Relations

What were to be the relations of the Soviet Union with the outside world?

Stalin's answer was expressed in the slogan 'socialism in one country'. He chose to concentrate on the task of securing the revolution in the USSR, regardless of what was happening to the Communist cause elsewhere. His perception of Russia's weakness and the consequent need for her to be always on the defensive led him to believe that this was the only policy available. The same perception underlay his decision to enforce industrialisation on the Soviet Union; unless this were undertaken he believed the capitalist West would move to destroy the Soviet Union: 'Either we do it or they will crush us.' International revolution was to be suspended indefinitely until the USSR had consolidated its own position beyond challenge. This was in direct conflict with the revolutionary internationalism of his great Bolshevik rival, Trotsky. Soviet foreign policy became essentially a matter of self-protection. A complication in this respect was that the USSR appeared to speak with two voices. The Comintern, the Moscow-based official mouthpiece of international Communism, continued to talk combatively of the Soviet Union leading the world towards violent revolution. In contrast, the Soviet Foreign Office under Stalin sought to develop diplomatic and commercial contacts with the very states and governments against whom the Comintern was directing its propaganda. The historian, J. N. Westwood, explains the USSR's inconsistent record on foreign relations in these terms:

1 [It] was caused by the dissonance between the People's Commissariat of Foreign Affairs and the activities of the Communist International. The former, like its Tsarist predecessor, was doing its best to promote Russia's interests within an existing world
5 order, whereas the latter stood for the destruction of that order.

*This ambiguity in Soviet attitudes created uncertainty and prevented Stalin and his country from ever being fully trusted abroad. Such distrust became increasingly important as a barrier to workable diplomatic or trade relations with the outside world. It is true that the USSR did enter into a number of commercial agreements in this period but these seldom proved lasting. Moreover, the diplomatic recognition formally accorded to the Soviet Union did little to lift the siege atmosphere that prevailed within the country. War scares were a recurrent feature of Soviet life under Stalin. In some respects these suited Stalin's domestic purposes; the threat of invasion justified the maintenance of his strict internal regime and made any expression of opposition appear like treachery. However, they were hardly calculated to present the USSR to foreign observers as a reliable partner with whom they could comfortably do business.

The rise of virulently anti-Bolshevik Nazism in Germany in the 1930s greatly increased the security needs of the USSR. Stalin's first move to nullify the threat was to attempt to negotiate defensive treaties with France and Britain. When those countries declined to respond, Stalin changed tactics and entered into the Nazi–Soviet non-aggression Pact of August 1939. The security he had won for the USSR by this diplomatic coup proved an illusion. Two years later, Hitler's armies launched their long-prepared invasion and the Soviet Union found itself engaged in a desperate struggle for survival.

*The USSR's eventual military victory in 1945 suggested that it was now a world power. Yet, even in triumph, Stalin's defensive attitude prevailed. The extraordinary suffering of the Soviet people in the war of 1941–45 became the great formative experience in modern Russian history. The devastation of so much of its territory, and the loss of 20 million of its people, intensified the Soviet Union's sense of isolation and vulnerability. After 1945, Stalin was even more determined to safeguard his country from any repetition of the foreign occupations that had occurred all too frequently since 1914. The outcome of the war gave him the means of ensuring this. The westward drive of the Soviet armies had left the USSR in control of large areas of Eastern Europe. Stalin now viewed these as buffer zones, guaranteeing Soviet security from the Western powers in general, and Germany in particular. His refusal to contemplate releasing the Soviet grip on these newly acquired regions was a factor in the development of the Cold War, the confrontation between Communist Eastern Europe and the Western democracies. Equally important in creating this East–West tension was the existence of nuclear weapons. Stalin had been disturbed by news of the USA's development of an atomic bomb in 1945; he had ordered that, regardless of the economic burden, the necessary resources and finance be placed at the disposal of Soviet scientists to enable them to produce a comparable Soviet weapon. In 1949 this was achieved. The arms-race had begun.

The Cold War, with its nuclear threat, its iron curtain dividing Eastern and Western Europe, and its spiralling arms race, was duly inherited by Khrushchev. He brought a fresh style to Soviet foreign policy. As part of his de-Stalinisation programme he followed a policy of co-existence with the West. Although this new Soviet approach was naturally welcomed by the West, the policy has to be seen in Soviet terms. For Khrushchev, co-existence was never simply or primarily a matter of good will. He conducted it because it seemed to offer the Soviet Union a way of lightening the heaviest of its economic burdens. The Cold War was highly expensive. Khrushchev knew that as long as it remained the dominant feature of East–West relations the Soviet Union would be crippled by heavy defence costs, preventing the recovery and expansion of the Soviet domestic economy. Khrushchev's oft-repeated promise that the USSR would in the near future overhaul the Western economies required that it free itself from the shackles imposed upon it by Stalin's restrictive industrial policies and adopt modern, expansive programmes. This could not be undertaken as long as international relations remained a matter of confrontation.

*Co-existence had its successes, but Khrushchev was faced by mounting problems in foreign relations. The division of Germany and

Berlin became increasingly embarrassing to the USSR. Encouraged by de-Stalinisation, the Eastern-bloc satellites showed dangerous signs of wanting their independence. China, under Mao Tse-tung, began to compete with the Soviet Union for the leadership of the Communist world. Opponents of Khrushchev within the Kremlin used these difficulties to attack his policies. They were provided with still stronger grounds for criticism in 1962; Khrushchev, having taken a Cold War gamble by installing nuclear missiles in Cuba, was forced to withdraw them when confronted by an American ultimatum. Despite his efforts to restructure Soviet foreign policy, Khrushchev left the USSR with as many problems as he had inherited. The pressing question that had confronted the USSR in 1924 – how could it guarantee its security in a hostile world? – was still unresolved in 1964.

In his memoirs, written in the late 1960s during his enforced retirement, Khrushchev claimed that his greatest contribution to the USSR as its leader had been in his role as international statesman. Despite his failures in foreign policy, this claim deserves attention. He had been the first Soviet leader to become widely known outside the USSR, personally representing his country in every continent. He had been one of the first statesmen in any country to develop 'summitry' as a standard form of international diplomacy. He had presided over the USSR's transition into a super-power, triumphantly watching it become the pioneer in space. He had been the first Soviet leader to declare that his country no longer thought in terms of an inevitable armed struggle between the forces of socialism and capitalism, and the first to recognise co-existence as a principle governing the relations between states. These were not inconsiderable achievements.

*Yet, during the 60 years since Lenin's death, little appeared to have changed. In 1924, the Soviet Union was an economically backward, internationally isolated, one-party state. In 1964, at the time of Khrushchev's fall, despite the prodigious effort and suffering of the people in the intervening years, the Soviet economy still lagged behind those of the advanced nations. Although a super-power, in control of Eastern Europe, the Soviet Union was locked in ideological struggle with both West and East. Internally it still remained subject to the rule of an intolerant and all powerful Communist Party that represented only 10% of the people. Despite its revolutionary origins, in 1964 the Soviet Union was a conservative society, suspicious of change. This was the enduring legacy of Stalinism.

Making notes on 'The Soviet Record, 1924–64'

Your notes on this chapter should be a review of the important features

1924   THE SOVIET RECORD   1964

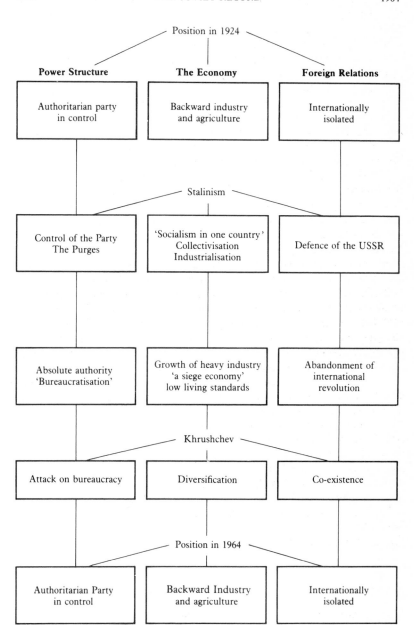

Summary – 'The Soviet Record, 1924–64'

of the period 1924–64 taken as a whole. They should be concerned with the aims and achievements of Stalin and Khrushchev in relation to the three key areas, political power, the economy and foreign relations. The following headings, sub-headings and questions should help you:

1   **Political Power**
1.1 The nature of Stalin's rule.
1.2 The main arguments on whether Stalinism was a development of Leninism.
1.3 How different was Khrushchev's position and use of power?

2   **The Soviet Economy**
2.1 Stalin's objectives. How progressive were they?
2.2 The debate on Stalin's methods.
2.3 How did Khrushchev attempt to redirect the Soviet economy?

3   **Foreign Relations**
3.1 What did 'Socialism in One Country' mean in foreign policy?
3.2 The USSR's emergence as a world power.
3.3 What did Khrushchev achieve by co-existence?

Answering essay questions on 'The Soviet Record, 1924–64'

To be able to answer questions that ask for an assessment of a whole period of Soviet history you must, of course, be familiar with the material in all the other chapters. A restricted or partial choice of study would make it difficult for you to make informed or adequate comment on the record overall. It is unlikely that you will ever be asked to write a narrative of the main developments between 1924 and 1964. However, you would be expected to know what happened and to be able to apply your factual knowledge to a range of general issues about Stalin and Khrushchev. Since modern Russian history is so controversial, you should make the effort to follow some of the major historical debates.

Obviously the three-theme approach in this chapter does not cover every aspect of the period, but it does direct attention to essentials. If you can master the developments relating to the power structure, the economy and foreign relations, you will have a sound base from which to comment intelligently. You may find the following list a useful way of approaching each of the themes:

Power
1 'Stalin's exercise of power in the Soviet Union destroyed more than it created.' Discuss.
2 Why was Khrushchev unable to exercise the same degree of power in the USSR that Stalin had?

Economy
3 Consider the view that 'Stalin's economic objectives could not have been achieved other than by the methods he used.'

4 'Stalin's economic policies, for all their brutality, were a success; Khrushchev's, for all their humanity, were a failure.' Discuss.

Foreign Policy

5 Was Soviet foreign policy under Stalin based on 'fear rather than aggression'?

6 What motives underlay Khrushchev's pursuit of a policy of co-existence with the West?

A-Level special study papers invariably include questions on historiography (the study of the way in which history is written and of how historians interpret evidence). It is good practice always to note down what you think is the attitude or bias of any writer or book that you may read on this subject. This is not always easy, but you will gain some clues by asking yourself direct questions, such as: Is he/she Marxist or non-Marxist? Is he/she an eye-witness or a later observer? Is he/she pro- or anti-Stalin, pro- or anti-Soviet? Typical examination questions are:

1 Why is there controversy among historians over the character of Stalin's leadership of the Soviet Union?

2 Did Stalin betray or fulfil the Revolution begun by Lenin?

Make a list of the main differences of interpretation regarding the link between Stalin and Lenin. Using this, look back over Chapters 1, 2 and 3 to check the things that Stalin said about his continuity with Lenin. Check also in Chapters 4 and 5 to remind yourself of the bearing of Stalin's economic and foreign policies on the issue of whether he continued or departed from Lenin's initiatives. You will find surveying the whole period, and the controversies relating to it, to be an interesting way to rethink and revise the particular topics that you studied in the previous chapters.

Source-based questions on 'The Soviet Record, 1924–64'

Stalinism

Read the extracts from the writings of Edward Crankshaw and Martin McCauley on pages 122 and 123, and then answer the following questions:

a) What does Crankshaw mean by saying (line 1) that 'Stalinism . . . was Leninism'?

b) Explain the reference in line 7 that 'Trotsky had good reason for presenting Stalin as an inferior'.

c) According to McCauley, what were the essential differences between Leninism and Stalinism?

d) As McCauley describes it, what place did the purges have in Stalin's exercise of power?

e) How would you explain the wide differences of opinion among historians in their interpretation of Stalinism?

Further Reading

You will not be surprised to learn that, in an area as significant as modern Soviet history, there are hundreds of excellent books. It is, of course, unrealistic to expect students to be able, within the limits of the normal A-Level course, to consult more than a few of these. However, it would be a pity to be too limited in your approach, particularly if you are taking the period as a special or depth study. Every year the reports of the A-Level Boards carry complaints that examinees do not read widely enough. The following suggestions are meant to serve as a guide.

J. N. Westwood, *Russia Since 1917* (Batsford, 1980)
As well as being a well-written study by a major scholar, this book has the great advantage of covering both the Stalin and the Khrushchev periods. It is a relatively short book, but it is safe to say that there is no important topic that it does not illuminate.

All historians acknowledge the debt they owe to E. H. Carr, whose life-long work on modern Russia, expressed in over 20 books, has set the standard for all subsequent research. Fortunately, he compressed many of his findings into one volume, written expressly, as he put it, 'for the student seeking a first introduction to the subject'.
E. H. Carr, *The Russian Revolution from Lenin to Stalin, 1917–29* (Macmillan, 1979)

Another very helpful paperback is:
Lionel Kochan, *The Making of Modern Russia* (Penguin, 1977)
The later chapters of this book cover the Stalin period up to 1945, and are especially informative on the economy and on foreign policy.

Of the large number of biographies of Stalin, arguably the most interesting is:
Isaac Deutscher, *Stalin: A Political Biography* (Penguin, 1970)
Despite its obvious bias, this portrait, painted by a supporter of Trotsky, is a fascinating introduction to the historical controversy over whether Stalin was the true heir of Lenin.

On that same vital theme another recommended text is:
Alec Nove, *Stalinism and After* (Allen and Unwin, 1975)
This has very good sections on both Stalin and Khrushchev, and puts both leaders in the context of Russian history since 1917. The same author has written the definitive work on the Soviet economy under Stalin and Khrushchev:
Alec Nove, *An Economic History of the USSR* (Penguin, 1972)

A distinguished scholar of Stalin's impact on the Soviet Union is:
Sheila Fitzpatrick. Her most accessible work is:
Sheila Fitzpatrick, *The Russian Revolution, 1917–32* (OUP, 1986)
As the dates suggest, the book is limited to the early years of Stalin's leadership, but the writer makes so many enlightened comments, and is so well informed on the work of her fellow historians that it makes her book a must.

A very readable book, which sets Stalin against the background of his time is:
Adam B. Ulam, *Stalin: The Man and His Era* (Allen Lane, 1974)

A notable study of Khrushchev is:
Edward Crankshaw, *Khrushchev: A Biography* (Sphere, 1968)
Crankshaw is interesting to the student because he is one of those Western historians who see a direct line of descent between Lenin, Stalin and Khrushchev. Despite de-Stalinisation, Crankshaw regards Khrushchev as in all essentials a Stalinist.

Students seeking detailed coverage of the post-1945 years are strongly urged to read:
Peter J. Mooney, *The Soviet Superpower: The Soviet Union, 1945–80* (Heinemann, 1982)

Glossary

Bolshevik   The name (meaning 'majority') taken by Lenin and his followers after the split in the SD Party in 1903. It was the Bolsheviks who seized power in the October Revolution of 1917.

Bourgeoisie   The Marxist term for the exploiting capitalist middle class against whom the industrial workers (the proletariat) were waging violent class war.

Central Committee (CC)   The chief executive body of the CPSU, responsible for shaping official Soviet policy.

Comintern   The Communist International organisation, established in 1919 for the purpose of bringing about revolution in other countries.

Commissar   Minister or key official in the Soviet government or CPSU.

CPSU   The Communist Party of the Soviet Union (formerly the Bolshevik Party).

DDR   The German Democratic Republic (East Germany).

FDR   The German Federal Republic (West Germany).

Kolkhozy   Collective farms set up as part of Stalin's enforced collectivisation of agriculture.

Komsomol   The Young Communist League, a movement for young people between the ages of 14 and 28, often enlisted for pioneer industrial or agricultural work.

Kulaks   Defined by Stalin as the class of rich peasants who had grown wealthy under the NEP and who must be destroyed as a prelude to collectivisation. Stalin asserted that the existence of the Kulaks would prevent the modernisation of the USSR.

Marxism-Leninism   Official Bolshevik/Communist ideology, based on the theories of Karl Marx as interpreted and practised by Lenin.

Menshevik   The word (meaning minority) used to describe the followers of Plekhanov after the split in the SD Party in 1903.

NEP   The New Economic Policy: the relaxing by Lenin in 1921 of the severe economic controls imposed during the Civil War. It reintroduced the market economy into agriculture and allowed the peasants to sell their surplus produce for private profit.

Nepmen   The class of merchants and middle-men who profited from the NEP.

NKVD   The initials of the state security police after 1935.

OGPU   The state security force which succeeded the *Cheka* as the body responsible for maintaining Bolshevik/Communist authority and control within the Soviet Union – renamed the NKVD in 1935.

Politburo   The Political Bureau, the highly-powerful inner cabinet of the Central Committee of the CPSU (known as the 'Presidium' between 1952 and 1966).

Pravda   The Russian word for truth, taken as the title of the official newspaper of the Bolshevik/CPSU Party.

Proletariat	The Marxist term for the revolutionary working class.
SDs	The Social-Democratic Workers' Party; the Marxist party which divided into Bolshevik and Menshevik wings in 1903.
Secretariat	The CPSU organisation which provided the officials, ministers and civil servants of the Soviet government. After Lenin's death it became Stalin's essential power-base.
Sovkhozy	State farms, introduced (along with the *Kolkhozy* in the late 1920s) as a way of collectivising the peasantry.
Sovnarkom	The Council of People's Commissars (the Government of the USSR).

Sources on 'Stalin and Khrushchev'

Although there are still certain areas within the period 1924–64 for which documents are difficult to find, a great deal of material has been published and translated since Stalin's death in 1953.

A valuable collection of extracts appears in:

Martin McCauley, *Stalin and Stalinism* (Longman, 1983)

What makes this a very helpful paperback for the student is the excellent accompanying commentary by the editor.

Another wide selection of documentary extracts, with linking comments, is provided by:

F. W. Stacey, *Stalin and the Making of Modern Russia* (Edward Arnold, 1970)

For primary-source material on collectivisation and the Purges, the student should consult the following, which contain copious documentary extracts:

Robert Conquest, *The Great Terror: Stalin's Purge of the Thirties* (Penguin, 1971)

Robert Conquest, *Harvest of Sorrow* (Macmillan, 1988)

A remarkable personal account of Stalin, written by his daughter, appears in:

Svetlana Alliluyeva, *Twenty Letters to a Friend* (Penguin, 1968)

The student would find it equally fascinating to dip into Khrushchev's memoirs. These insights into the ideas and policies of both Stalin and Khrushchev are published in English as:

N. S. Khrushchev, *Khrushchev Remembers* (Andre Deutsch, 1971)

The Soviet emigre, Solzhenitsyn, has drawn on his own personal experience, to write a multi-volume work, describing life in Stalin's labour camps. Any part of this is worth reading:

Alexander Solzhenitsyn, *The Gulag Archipelago* (Collins, 1974–78)

Another personal testament by a Russian writer who also suffered under Stalin, but, unlike Solzhenitsyn, remained loyal to the USSR is:

R. A. Medvedev, *Let History Judge* (Macmillan, 1973)

Index

Alliluyeva, S 63–4
Anti-Comintern Pact 78

Beria, L 55, 96
Brezhnev, L 115
Bukharin, N 16, 21–5, 57–9, 100
Bulganin, N 96–8, 107

Castro, F 112
Chiang Kai-shek 74, 79, 86
Constitution of USSR (1936) 59, 78

Hitler, A 71, 77–80, 84
Homo Sovieticus 37

Kagonovich, L 23, 98, 117
Kamenev, L 9, 14–17, 20–1, 55, 57
Kennedy, J 108, 110
Kirov, S 21, 53–5, 57, 67–8
Kolkhozy 28
Kosygin, A 115
Kulaks 30–2, 48

Lenin, V 1, 5, 13–14, 15, 25, 29, 70,
  101, 107, 114, 122
Lenin's *Testament* 15
Litvinov, M 77, 80

Magnitogorsk 37–8, 50
Malenkov, G 96–8, 105
Malinovsky, R 98
Mao Tse-tung 74–5, 113–15, 130
Marshall Plan 88–9, 94, 108
Marxism 1, 13, 29, 101, 107, 114,
  122
Mensheviks 12, 20, 55
Molotov, V 21, 58, 80, 96, 98, 117

Nagy, I 103
NKVD 56, 60

OGPU 40
Orgburo 12

Pilsudski, J 75
Plekhanov, G 8

Politburo 12, 57
Poskrebyshev, A 55
Potsdam Conference 62, 85–7
Pravda 9, 22, 96, 115–16
Preobrazhensky, M 29
Pyatakov, Y 58

Radek, K 58
Rapallo, Treaty of 71, 75
Riyutin, M 52–3
Rykov, A 14, 21–2, 24, 57

Secretariat 11, 55
Serge, V 54
Shakhty trial 38
Smirnov, A 15
Sokolnikov, G 58
Solzhenitsyn, A 123
Sovkhozy 28
Spanish Civil War 79
'Sputnik' 107
Stakhanov, A 42

Tito, J 102
Tomsky, N 14, 21–2, 24, 57–8
Trotsky, L 9, 12, 15–19, 21–2, 42,
  56–8, 74–5, 100, 128
'Truman Doctrine' 88–9
Tukhachevsky, M 60

Uglanov, N 23
Ulbricht, W 110–111

Voroshilov, K 60
Vyshinsky, A 55, 57–9, 89

Warsaw Pact 103

Yagoda, N 55, 57
Yalta Conference 62, 85–7, 108
Yezhov, N 55, 58
Yorykin, A 65

Zhdanov, A 55
Zhukov, G 96, 98
Zinoviev, G 9, 14–17, 20–1, 55, 57
'Zinoviev Letter' 72–3, 93